To the Cleveland Station

To the One who stood beside me

TO THE CLEVELAND STATION

Carol Anne Douglas

THE NAIAD PRESS INC.
1982

Printed in the United States of America
First Edition

Cover design and title page by Tee A. Corinne

Typesetting by C & H Publishing Services
Shelburne Falls, Massachusetts

Library of Congress Cataloging in Publication Data

Douglas, Carol Anne.
    To the Cleveland Station.

    I. Title.
PS3554.08235T6   813'.54   81-22449
ISBN 0-930044-27-4   AACR2

About the Author:

Carol Anne Douglas is a lesbian feminist / radical feminist who has been active in the feminist movement since 1972. She has worked on the feminist newspaper *off our backs* since 1973, and says that the paper is the mainstay of her life and the women on the newspaper collective "get better and better every year." Her short novel, *Mary Anti-Mary,* was printed by *off our backs* in 1973, and a book of her poems, *Loving Women Is Dangerous,* was published in 1977.

To Cindy,

Love, Bad

To the Cleveland Station

1

I am not allowed to go to Cleveland. You might wonder why I care. How many people would consider themselves in exile if Cleveland were their Eden, their Jerusalem? Whenever I see the name "Cleveland"—when the city's baseball team gets mentioned, when Grover Cleveland's name comes up (you'd be surprised how often a name comes up if you want to avoid those syllables), when the mayor makes national news—I cringe. The name hurts. (Not to mention the fact that I, like Walter Mondale, live in a part of Washington called Cleveland Park—but Walter Mondale is not a dyke in a two-hundred dollar a month, roach-infested apartment with faucets that have leaked for two years.)

Well, I've been happier in Cleveland than anywhere else in my life. Perhaps that says something about Cleveland, perhaps it says more about my life. There are explanations for this—since I am one who is obsessed with explanations. I explain why I don't like the rain, why I still eat meat, why I don't like pop art, why I do like some authors even though they are men (I explain this *before* I am challenged)—so, naturally, it will take me a whole book to say why I am not allowed in Cleveland. An explanation is something like an apology—one of my standard jokes is that if I wrote an autobiography it would have to be titled *I'm Sorry* because I say "I'm sorry" so often.

My name is Brenda Anne Dougherty. I have been a radical feminist since the early seventies. I don't like to admit the exact date because I am embarrassed that I wasn't one of the early feminists. I never get into social movements quickly enough to feel good about myself. There may be ways that I'm original, but that isn't one of them. In my arrogance, the first thing I did when I heard about feminism was not to read about it (which would be a logical thing for a woman with a master's degree in political science who considered herself a radical intellectual to do) or to join an organization: oh, no, I wrote a novel about how the Virgin Mary would have felt if she had been a feminist—without ever picking up the smallest feminist pamphlet until after I had finished. As I said, I am arrogant, sometimes much more arrogant than I realize. Oh, well, a little arrogance can be fun.

I have worked since 1973 on a feminist newspaper (which I adamantly refer to as a *radical feminist* newspaper, meaning something very particular and very doctrinaire, which nobody else calls it so insistently). The newspaper is called *Womanpaper* and is located in Washington, D.C., about ten blocks from the White House, going north along Connecticut Avenue. We busily pretend that we are not located so close to the seat of male power, and hardly ever write about it. (Well, I am a bit of a renegade about this—I have actually done some lobbying and am fascinated by Congress. I read about American politics for entertainment. Watergate helped me through many a crisis. Why, for the last two years of my marriage there was nothing to talk about *but* Watergate.)

The newspaper is wonderful. Really. You can actually write and see your own words in print a few days later. Not all of the words are perfectly chosen—we rush so fast. My news stories aren't the world's best. The first story I wrote was so dreadful—I was supposed to write an expose of the National Women's Political Caucus but I couldn't bring myself to do it (they were feminists too). Besides, every woman I interviewed told me that what she said was confidential. I never know in advance whether an article is just right or an awful mistake—most of us are probably the same in that way. But we put out the silly paper, the incredibly wonderful paper, month after month, year after year.

Although I may in many ways appear to be the most predictable and puritanical of lesbian feminists, I am a compulsive gambler and always play long-shots. Choosing to be a lesbian feminist in the first place is, after all, a bit of a gamble. (My puritanism forces me to inform you hastily that I do not gamble with money. Only with my life.)

In the beginning of the seventies, I had a nice, relatively handsome (at least as good-looking as I) nuclear physicist husband, who did more than half of the housework, was an excellent cook, put my career ahead of his, supported me through most of graduate school, encouraged my radical feminist activism, and so, I supposed, loved me. Now I am a lesbian feminist and will remain one if I never make love with another woman.

Let me start right out by stating that I loved my mother and hated my father. That is open, that is a given. Let the therapist who told me, "You hate these men like Hitler, George Wallace, rapists, etcetera, because they remind you of your father," have her say and be done with it. If the therapist assumes that the statement only reveals something about me and not about the political condition of the world or of men, let her.

I spent little time defying my father—no doubt I would be a more effective feminist had I rebelled against him more. I discovered that there was another kind of person—my mother. And I must admit that I preferred supporting women to defying men—which, of course, has led me to become a lesbian but doesn't always do much for my feminism. I believe that demonstrations are more effective than love affairs or writing about them—but I can hardly tear the pen out of my hands and have certainly spent more time trying to understand lovers than marching in the streets. Yet I want the world to change for *all* women, not just those I happen to meet or to love. I want to contribute more than kisses and poetry—after all, men have kissed women and written about them for a good long time, and I'm not terribly pleased with the results.

When I was fourteen, I read a review of the movie of *The Children's Hour,* and knew that was *me.* I heard all sorts of delicious rumors about lesbianism in girls' schools, but I was in a Catholic girls' school and there was nary a lesbian in sight, although numerous girls seemed to have "crushes" on nuns and on each other. When the most tomboyish girl in school started dating, I assumed that this course was inevitable—I too must look for a man. I was somewhat physically attracted to men, I liked some of them—I just didn't fall in love in quite the same way that I did with women.

This is not a story about my relationships with men. There weren't many. One hysterical foolishness, a few brief dates, and one marriage that wasn't too awful—I certainly wouldn't have left him for another man. I carefully chose a man who was relatively gentle, considerate, and as little like my father as I could possibly find. There are times when I can hardly believe that I could have left such a person. That is, I thought he was a person. I thought that we could be persons together and live in a quiet, serious person-world.

But this is not a personworld. Men and women are treated differently. His experiences and his feelings were different from mine. I kept wishing he was a woman.

I "fell in love" again soon, with the feminist movement. The moment I walked into a feminist meeting—about six months after I got married—I was in love, permanently in love. (I'm generally pretty good at telling the difference between my permanent commitments and my temporary ones, if I am being honest—my cat, for instance, has always been a permanent commitment. It was somewhat embarrassing to realize that I had a more permanent commitment to my cat than to my husband, but cats being what they are and people being what they are, it certainly has been easier. After seven and a half years, Mouse and I are still together.)

Of course, nothing could be more anti-feminist than using a phrase like "permanently in love." Ti-Grace Atkinson, whom I admire for being metaphysical and for using words like "metaphysical" (I love philosophical language though I may tend to use it pompously) has defined "love" as "the response that the victim gives to the oppressor." Under that definition, my use of the word "love" to describe my feelings for the feminist movement has, of course, no meaning. But I love (I choose the word deliberately) some of the ordinary language of American women, though it reflects their oppressed state. I like to call certain kinds of people "cute" and "adorable," and I hope that I will remember not to use those words in front of women who will shudder. I want to use the word "love" to express what I perceive to be a serious emotional commitment, persisting through time and varying from hysterical passion to worry to thoughtful, day-to-day support, but giving guidance and form (or content) to one's life. By that definition, I love the feminist movement. I read all her works, theoretical and literary, and try to keep up with all her progress and backsliding, her tensions, feuds, and righteous confrontations, her humor and the dangers that may lie in wait for her in the world out there that wants to tame and assimilate her.

I am an ex-Catholic who looked for another faith and found it. That explains so much about me. Being an ex-Catholic makes me a bit skeptical of my faith, but more skeptical of the idea that nothing is worth believing in.

In the beginning of 1974, I stopped sleeping with Ted, my

husband. It was not at all hard to do. I never wanted to embrace him again. I told him that I wanted to take a break from the pill, but I knew that I was really cutting him off. Later that year, I approached a woman friend I loved, but was rejected. When I went home and cried, Ted comforted me. He wanted me to be a bisexual, to do anything if I would only stay. But I knew that women would feel unable to trust me if I were bisexual.

I told Ted that I would leave him eventually to live my life as a lesbian. He cried and felt pains in his chest. I went with him to the emergency room, to be sure that the pains weren't a heart attack. They weren't. Some women on the newspaper were disgusted with me for being so sympathetic to him, and I was disgusted with them. They had left old-style husbands—they didn't understand that leaving a new-style one was harder.

Besides, I knew how he felt because I had once been in love with a black man who married a black woman. The idea that you are left for someone more "relevant" or that you are permanently excluded from the other person's group no matter how much good will you think you have is incredibly frustrating.

I was terrified of leaving him. Perhaps I could stay with him and be celibate. What if no one else loved me. I wasn't sure that a woman could.

This story begins in early 1975. I shall abandon saying "I" simply because the book is *so* egocentric that I would have to use it ten thousand times—you would scream if you had to read it that often.

This is the story of how radical feminist Brenda Anne Dougherty became a lesbian feminist. It does not pretend to be an objective picture of her relationship or an objective herstory of *Womanpaper:* the story only presents Brenda's experience. I laugh about it because it is still so close.

2

One day Brenda walked into the newspaper office—two shabby rooms that she loved much, decorated only with political posters —and looked through the log in which were recorded the minutes of the collective's meeting. Important notices and interesting letters and manuscripts were sometimes put in the log. She found a letter written on yellow legal paper in shaky handwriting.

Dear Newspaper Collective,

Your newspaper is great. I had to write to tell you how much I like it and how brave I think you are for being so open and out as lesbians. Women like you are changing many things.

I'm not like you. I'm afraid to come out. I am proud to be a lesbian. I've been a lesbian all my life (I'm twenty-six, black, and I live in Cleveland). I can't imagine being anything else.

Why don't people understand how much women love each other? Why can't they see it's beautiful? Why are they so full of hate? I am in the closet. My family hates "bull daggers." I can't tell them. They don't understand. I feel so bad not being able to tell them.

I work with so-called community workers, but gays aren't part of their community. There are many jokes about faggots and a gay man was fired a few weeks ago for being gay. I'm so afraid that they'll find out about me, but I hate myself for being cowardly and not telling them who I really am. I keep thinking they might find out anyway.

The churches don't accept us either. Nobody accepts us. Why can't they see that we are just people, trying to be good and love each other? Some of us believe in God just as much as anybody else does. For a while we had an MCC (Metropolitan Community Church) here, and I used to go to that, but that closed down and there is nowhere to go.

My long-time lover died last year, and I have been alone. Our life together was very beautiful. But we lived in the suburbs and didn't know many other gay women. I feel so alone now.

I tried joining NOW, but they never said anything about lesbians. I don't like to go to the bars. The women in this town are too much into roles, and I'm not interested in that.

I wish I could be brave and open like you, but it is too hard. I can't keep it up any longer. I want to die. It would be better to be a stronger person, but I'm not. I'd rather die than keep on hiding and being alone.

Keep on doing your work. You are brave and I'm proud to know there are women like you.

Andy

Brenda was very aware of not being a proper lesbian. She had not officially come out or touched a woman with tongue, but she believed in lesbianism thoroughly and wanted to be a lesbian, wrote poems about women, hoped not to be denounced as some kind of married bisexual dreadful. Torquemada in all his fury could not have been in more of a holy rage than she was when she discovered this message lying in the logbook among the announcements of women's art shows and the subscription agency library shows, asking whether the collective wanted to pay $145 for a display table, all waiting for the Thursday night meeting. This was Monday—Andy could be dead by then. She could be dead by now. But she might be planning to do it between now and then, might want somebody to stop her—or else why send a message?

She read the letter thoroughly again, trying to find clues. The postmark was from a small town outside Cleveland, not from Cleveland itself. The only clues she could find were the references to the local NOW chapter and to the gay church group.

She dialed Cleveland information and called the NOW chapter. Amazingly, there was someone in the office.

"Pardon me, but I'm with the feminist newspaper *Womanpaper* in Washington, D.C. We're (the "I" quickly became "we") trying to find a woman who wrote us. She's young, black, named Andy, and lives in Cleveland. Do you know her? We need to reach her."

"No," said the woman at the other end, sounding a little puzzled. "I don't know anybody like that."

"Do you know anybody who might know? It's really quite important."

She was dubious, but gave some names and phone numbers of NOW members.

"Do you know of any gay church in the area? Apparently she belonged to that."

"No, I don't. I'm sorry." She didn't seem too sorry to get off the phone.

Brenda called the three numbers she had been given. Three "no answers." Probably all home numbers for working women.

She went to the filing cabinet and hunted through the files where subscribers' names were kept in zip code order. Not surprisingly, none of the Cleveland area subscribers were named Andy or Andrea. Either she used another name or she bought the paper in a store. There were no subscribers in Fenwick, the small town or suburb on the postmark. She called every one of the subscribers in the area—about fifteen. Five had no phone number listed for that name, four had phone numbers and were home. None of them had ever heard of Andy. She asked them whether there were any women's or gay groups in the town that she could talk to. One woman called back with the numbers of two feminist groups and one gay group. She called them, found out that the gay church was indeed dispersed and the minister had left town.

Brenda was becoming more frantic. She started admitting that she was calling about someone who had sent a suicide note. From the groups came the names of more groups. More people said they would call back if they got numbers or information. It was now after five. (Hope the collective didn't mind all of this calling before five—the hell with them if they minded. A life was at stake. Why hadn't the first person who saw the letter done this very thing—it must have come in today's mail—why wasn't she still here?) So she started calling the numbers of people who hadn't been home during the day. Call. Call. Dial. Dial. She wasn't getting any-where—was there some vital thing she should be doing that she hadn't thought of? What was *she* doing now? Had *she* slit her wrists or thrown herself in front of a car? Was *she* dead or in a hospital? Or was *she* just going about her ordinary life, unhappy? Or had *she* taken pills, or was *she* taking a long time to die?

Brenda decided to call her karate teacher—not because she was adamant about people showing up for class (which she was) but be-cause she was going to drive Brenda there. (Her karate teacher, Lee Jasur, was an early ('68) radical feminist, obsessed with self-defense as she was with feminism, almost to the point of believing that the two are synonymous. She was a quiet, small person with great dignity. Brenda had never been able to prod her to talk about personal matters, though she'd tried. Lee was, in both her written feminist theory and her life, a celibate.)

Lee answered the phone. By this point, Brenda was terribly

grateful to anybody who answered the phone. "I don't think I can come to class tonight. We got this suicide note at the paper from a woman in Cleveland and I've been trying to find her. I've been calling and calling groups and subscribers in Cleveland for hours. I've got to stay here."

"I think you should come to class," said Lee. "Karate is good for calming you down when you're upset."

"No, it's not just that I'm upset. This is important. You don't understand. I've got to reach her."

"I think you should come to karate. You need to get away from this." Her voice had the same firm, calm timbre as in class. Brenda was pleased at the attention, but annoyed that Lee was so narrow.

"Karate isn't the only thing in the world. I'm staying here." Brenda's voice was not calm and firm in timbre.

"I'll be there in half an hour to pick you up. You can't do any more tonight. You can continue tomorrow." She hung up.

Brenda was pleased at this attention from the famous and admirable Lee. Lee was personally ordering her to class and coming to take her there! But she was also annoyed that Lee did not immediately give up everything and join her in her search. Brenda felt that she was too alone, that nobody else cared, and she was angry. Nobody else had come into the office all afternoon. She wished there was someone to relieve her. She called a couple of friends, but they weren't home. She debated refusing to go with Lee. But after another half hour of calls, Brenda was exhausted and had pretty well run through her list of home phone numbers.

On the way to karate class, Brenda tried to describe the letter to Lee.

"We can't help everybody," Lee said, in the usual expressionless tone. "We have to concentrate on the people who can help themselves. We can't spend all our time taking care of the others. If you're going to make a revolution, you can't exhaust yourself that way."

Brenda was furious—and was confirmed in her belief that Lee was one-sided. "Some of the finest people I've known have tried to kill themselves. You're wrong. We can't just concentrate on supposedly 'together' people. All of us have problems."

The next day, the calls continued until she exhausted the numbers and wasn't getting any more referrals. She was defeated, and still angry.

Thursday night Brenda opened the meeting angrily. (This was perhaps the only time in Brenda's years in the movement that she had started an angry scene in a meeting so provocatively.)

"Who opened the letter?" she demanded. (This was not her usual style.) "Why was it just stuck in the log? Why didn't anybody try to do anything until I found it? I've been calling Cleveland all week and I can't find her."

Shana, a woman Brenda was none too fond of (she tended to be closer to people in anti-imperialist groups than in other feminist groups, and to write more about imperialism than male supremacy, which was quite enough to prevent Brenda from being fond of her) said that she had opened the letter but had thought "it didn't really sound like the woman who wrote it was going to kill herself."

"Where did you ever get that idea? How did you know?" Brenda was livid.

"It sounds more like she just wanted to express her feelings."

"Let's pass the letter around and see," somebody else said. Which they did. The consensus of those who deigned to read it—and not everyone could have read it thoroughly, Brenda thought, judging from the time they took—was that it was not a suicide note. She was not going to kill herself. Brenda did not change her mind.

Someone suggested—perhaps to mollify Brenda—that they print an appeal to her to get in touch with them. They debated whether to put it in the classified ads or on the letters page. "Everyone reads letters," somebody said. "We should put it on the letters page." Brenda agreed.

When they put out their next paper a week later, Brenda wrote a letter saying, "Dear Andy, We are worried about you. Please get in touch with us," and put it on the top of the first page of letters, with a headline saying "andy" in twenty-four point medium type. Brenda didn't expect a response. She thought the chances that Andy was dead were about fifty-fifty.

Brenda thought about Nina, her closest friend on the paper, who had attempted suicide a year and a half before. How different the collective's reactions had been then! They had realized that preserving Nina was more important than any of their other work, was a precondition for any other work.

3

Two weeks later, a woman on the collective told Brenda that Andy had called. "I couldn't handle it," she said. "I told her to call back when you were here. I guess you want to talk to her."

"Of course I do." Brenda hung around the office waiting for the call.

"Hello, I'm Andy. Are you Brenda Anne? I heard you were the woman who was looking for me." The voice was soft and deep.

"Hello. Are you all right?" Brenda didn't know what to say, but she wanted to say it right.

"I am now" (emphasis on the "now").

"Your letter really got to me. Did you try . . . ?"

"Lucky me. I tried, but didn't get too far. I tried playing in traffic, but I just got a broken leg."

"I knew you'd try. Nobody else believed it, but I knew. Are you okay? How's your leg?"

"My little leg is doing just fine. I couldn't believe it when I saw my name in your paper. I didn't think anybody would notice the letter."

"Not *notice* it? I was calling every one of our subscribers in Cleveland. You aren't a subscriber, or the name Andy isn't on your subscription."

"True. Aren't you the detective?" This was said very warmly. "You really did that?"

"My God, of course I did. I was worried to death. I called every women's or gay organization in Cleveland."

"You did that because of a *letter*? I can't believe you did all that." But her tone was full of affection.

Brenda enjoyed the affection. "What else could I do? But how are you feeling now? I mean, really."

"Oh, I'm okay. I'm not going to do anything fancy now with my leg like this."

"Are the things that made you feel so bad any different, if I might ask?"

"Of course you can ask. Who has a better right? If you want to hear. Things aren't any different. My lover died last summer, and I'm alone. Nobody knows how I feel. I work with a bunch of liberal lawyers who make a big deal about how much they're for the community, but they talk about faggots and they just fired a couple of guys for being faggots. I was scared. What if they guessed about me? But there isn't anybody for them to guess about. I know what I am, but how can you be gay if you don't have a lover? I don't think I'll ever love anybody again that way. So why do I have to hide being gay? What do I have to hide?"

"Oh, Andy, that's so terrible. I'm sorry. Listen, I don't have a lover now myself, but that doesn't make me any less lesbian. It sounds like you've been through a lot."

"Yeah. A lot."

"How long were you with her?"

"Five years."

"That's a long time."

"Not long enough. She—Maxy—Maxy was . . . Why am I telling you all this? Do you really want to hear it?"

"Yes, very much, if you want to tell. I like to talk about personal things."

"A stranger like you and you want to hear it? That blows my mind." The voice was still soft. "Most people I know I wouldn't tell. Only a few gay ones. And I don't tell them anything."

"It's okay, I'm a lesbian too." Brenda Anne was political enough to use the word "lesbian" rather than "gay" and hope that it affected everyone's consciousness. It should not be seen as a scary word.

"Do you tell everybody?"

"I'm lucky. I work here at *Womanpaper* and I don't have a straight job. So just about all of the people I usually see know that I'm a lesbian. My straight friends are feminists, so that's no problem. I haven't told my family yet, but most of them are in California." Brenda decided that she wouldn't tell Andy that she hadn't slept with a woman yet, not to mention that she was still living, though chastely, with a husband. Brenda believed that those facts were less important than her determination to become a lesbian and her belief in the desirability of lesbianism. The facts would simply cloud the issue and make it difficult for the other woman to trust her; she was quite sure that she ought to be trusted.

"Oh, my family. I don't even like to think about what it would do to my family. I'm living with my grandmother now and she'd tell me to get out. She doesn't care for dykes at all."

"Living with your grandmother? That must be hard, even having to hide things from people you live with."

"I'm clever. I hide them well." Andy giggled. "I keep all my lesbian books and stuff in a locked drawer and I hide it away whenever I think she's coming near my room. I used to have a place with Maxy, but since she died I haven't wanted to live alone."

"That's really hard. I understand the feeling, but it would be pretty rough if you always lived some place where you needed to hide. You're going through a lot of heavy things I've never had to deal with. No wonder you get down."

"Down? Oh, not little Andy! Where did you ever get that idea? Why, I'm just the cheerfullest person you would ever want to see." Her voice was pitched high, cute and bubbling.

"Just the happiest person who ever sent a suicide note?"

"You guessed it," chortled Andy.

"I'm deeply impressed by your happiness." How far did she dare go with this humor?

"Glad I've impressed you. I wouldn't want you to worry or get the notion that anything was wrong."

"Me? Worry? Oh certainly not. I'll only worry about you about twenty times a day."

"Now, why would you want to spend your time doing that? Worrying about a stranger like me?"

"I don't have anything better to do."

"A newspaper writer like you? I'm sure."

"You will give me a call sometime and let me know how you're doing?"

"Of course I will, newspaper woman."

Saturday morning was one of Brenda's less favorite mornings. Weekdays were much better. On Saturdays and Sundays she woke up beside Ted, but on weekdays he would be on his way to work before she rose.

She loathed the feeling of being just a few inches from someone she didn't want to touch and was always a little afraid that he would reach out across the several-inch barrier she tried to maintain even when she was sleeping. She could easily stop him by a word: that wasn't the problem. She didn't want to keep saying no; it was so much easier if he never asked. He rarely did, anymore.

At times she almost wished that she was still attracted to him. Ted seemed the essence of security. Yes, yes, she knew that the "exceptional man" was a myth. She believed that she was reinforcing the psychological strength of the patriarchy if she even walked down the street with him. Much better to always walk with women. Although she hadn't read Kant, she had heard of Kant's "categorical imperative" and thought it was a fine idea. Don't do anything unless you'd want other people in the same situation to do the same thing. She didn't believe that men could possibly be of much assistance to women (as a group) now. So the minute a woman walking by the Women's Liberation office in 1972 saw her wedding ring and said, "Oh, you can have feminism and a husband, too," Brenda had taken off her ring and kept it off.

But here she was in 1975 still in bed with Ted, the only progress being the several inches of space between them. Three inches in three years: not very impressive. At that rate, it would take longer than their lifetimes to get him out of the front door. She still wasn't sure whether she'd ever be able to go that far.

Last year, when Brenda had proposed to a woman she loved and had been turned down, Ted was the one who comforted her when the tears came—Brenda, of course, was incapable of hiding anything, of refraining from telling him. They weren't swingers: neither one of them had had "sexual intercourse" with anyone but the other—strange in 1970 America, they had been virgins in their middle twenties when they married. That was precisely why she had wanted him—because he wasn't sexually aggressive, wouldn't use women.

But have I used him, she worried. He snored. He looked just the littlest bit like Cary Grant—well, now with long hair and a beard, he looked like Cary Grant playing Jesus. He was good-looking enough, certainly. She just wished that a certain not particularly beautiful but somehow splendid woman were lying beside her instead. Was that always the universal game: "A" loves "B" who loves "C"? Intolerable. What a stupid joke on everyone.

She closed her eyes as she heard him rustling around. He got up, put on his robe (a shining blue velour she had given him when they were engaged), got the Washington *Post*, skimmed it, went to the bathroom, got dressed, and left for his Saturday hike along the Potomac. During the whole operation, she pretended to sleep, only allowing herself to stir when he was in the living room or the bathroom. She felt guilty for hiding but resented him, as if he was forcing the game on her.

Only Ted would be crazy enough to go hiking on the Potomac in this weather. (She should have realized what he'd be like, since their first date was a hike that started at 5 a.m.) She wanted him out of the apartment so she could study. He had a Ph.D. himself, but he wasn't the kind of person who would study quietly all day as she did—he'd be jumping up every little while to bake a cake, repair a window, or go to some store for some essential gear or cooking oil.

Brenda was supposed to take her Ph.D exams in political theory in a few weeks. She put on her robe, petted the cat and fed him (something Ted never managed to do), got a coke (her substitute for coffee) out of the refrigerator, and looked through her stack of theory books. Too bad she'd already finished re-reading Plato for the fifth time. Aristotle next, damnit. Old windbag. Some nerve calling himself a student of Plato's. Really believed that an owner had superior virtue to a slave. Just like Confucius. Who could be anything but an idealist, like Plato? Of course there's an ideal table somewhere. Of course there's an ideal feminist somewhere—we have a concept to strive for. Of course I can say I'm a lesbian, meaning that I have accepted the idea of lesbianism and am trying to achieve the reality. But aren't I a lesbian before I perform any concrete, physical act? The Catholic Church says you can become a Catholic by baptism of desire if regular baptism isn't available. So I'm a lesbian by baptism of desire.

The phone rang. She wasn't getting anything done. She'd only read a paragraph of Aristotle. She made her way back to the bedroom of the two-room apartment and picked up the phone.

"Hello," said a familiar voice. "Is this Miss Brenda Anne Dougherty?"

"Andy! Hello. How are you?" She was extremely surprised.

"Oh, couldn't be better. My one leg is dancing around with joy. And how are you this Saturday morning? Hope I didn't wake you up?"

"No, I'm just fine. I was studying."

"Studying? You're a student, too?"

"I'm trying to get a Ph.D. in political science."

"Of course you are. You're just a genius, that's all."

Brenda giggled uncomfortably. "Sure. Thanks for the compliment, although calling me Saturday morning is an even nicer compliment. You're sounding good."

"Of course I'm sounding good. Who do you think I am, some kind of gloomy person? I couldn't think of anyone I'd rather call."

"Compliments, compliments. You're turning my head."

"Don't mention it. I hope my call doesn't bother you."

"Are you kidding? It's fun. You are definitely more fun than Aristotle."

"Of course I am. That's me, the fun kid. But maybe someone like you thinks Aristotle is more fun."

"Plato, maybe. Aristotle, no way. He was not a very lively guy."

"A dull dude, eh? Does that make him any different from most other dudes?"

They both giggled.

"Well, maybe I'll bother you again sometime."

"Anytime. Please! Especially when I'm reading this stuff."

On Monday afternoon the phone rang again.

"Hello. Just wanted to see how you were doing?" The voice was duller, with a trace of irony.

"I'm fine—if anyone who has to read St. Augustine's *City of God* can be called fine."

"City of God you say? Sounds like where I'm headed—can't be any worse than here."

Every muscle in Brenda's body tensed. "Sure it can. Things can always get worse. What's worse about today than Saturday?"

"Nothing much. I'm just less foolish. Maybe I shouldn't have called you. You won't want to hear."

"Of course you should. I do want to hear."

"That's because you don't know me."

"Sure I know you. 'Getting to know you ... getting to like you ... '" Brenda warbled. Her voice cracked and squeaked, far off-key — which was not far from her best singing voice. "Pardon the showing off. I just wanted to impress you with my exquisite voice."

"Please! My ears! I've got very sensitive hearing. You're a writer. You're a scholar. But don't ever believe that you're a singer, honey."

"Sorry you don't appreciate my golden chords."

"Well, at least I know I'm not in heaven yet, because the angels wouldn't dare sing like that. Thanks for cheering me up. Maybe I should go now."

"Excuse me if I'm being pushy, but are you okay? I can keep talking."

"You're pushy, but I like it. If you're foolish enough to want to listen to me, I guess I'm foolish enough to talk to you. I guess the pills can wait."

Brenda was frozen. Let me say the right thing. "Do you have pills with you now?" She tried to make her voice sound natural.

"Oh just a little bottle in my hand. Sleeping pills."

"What kind?"

"Prescription. Those others aren't any good. Don't worry, I shouldn't have told you. I probably won't do anything."

"I hope not. Would you throw them away—put them down the toilet?"

"No, you don't. Then I couldn't take them. Don't worry. I just want to have them around."

"Oh, of course. Everybody likes to keep pills around—in their hand."

"Sure they do."

"What's the matter today, anyway? What's happened?"

"Nothing much."

"Where did nothing much happen, if you don't mind my asking?"

"At the office. They told more jokes about dykes and faggots."

"You're going to kill yourself because they told some jokes?"

"Sure. Why not? That's my little dyke joke."

"Oh, it's hilarious. Can't you hear me laughing?"

More softly, Andy said, "No, I can't. I shouldn't have told you. I don't want to worry you. I'm not worth worrying about."

"Sure you are."

"No, I'm not. I'm a traitor. When they say those things about bull-dykes, I have to joke, too, so they won't think I'm one. See, I'm not like you. I'm not worth your time."

"Yes, you are, damnit. Of course it's not great that you joined in their joking, but it's not worth dying over."

"Yes, it is. I'm so afraid of letting anyone know what I am that I'll betray Maxy and everything. Funny kid. I'm not so great."

"Of course you're scared after those guys lost their jobs. But wouldn't it be possible—I don't know, because I don't know what the people there are like—wouldn't it be possible sometime to say that jokes about gays aren't that cool without having people think you're gay yourself? Surely there must be some straight people who do that—I know a few."

"I don't know. I don't think I could. Like I said, I get afraid. That's why I tried to kill myself before—because I was a traitor."

"A joke isn't worth dying over."

"It's not a joke—it's my whole life. What is there to live for? I'm not going to do anything wonderful for anybody."

"Why not? You're a legal aid worker. Doesn't that help people?"

"Sure, that way. But I'm not a good person."

"As far as I can tell, you're plenty good."

"Sure I am. Betraying everything I am for some jerks at the office."

"Well, you've been through a lot. And you're lonely. But you could try—if not now, someday—to go places where you might meet some nice young lesbian."

"It's no good. I'm never going to feel that way again. I might as well meet some nice young pills."

"So why meet them today? I'm not saying that life is great, damnit. It is perfectly possible that you may decide that life is so bad that suicide is the only proper response to it—but there's no reason why you have to do that today. You're still in your twenties. Virginia Woolf decided that when she was forty-five or fifty, something like that. Why not live awhile longer before you make that decision? You can always commit suicide anytime, but you can't always take back the decision. Why not wait a little longer?"

"You do have a point. I can always do it. How'd you ever think of that?"

"That's what I tell myself."

"Really? You too?"

"Of course I've had suicidal feelings. That's why I was so struck by your note. That's why I care about you—besides the fact that I like you."

"You like me, do you?"

"Yes, I like you."

"I like you too. Okay, maybe I'll wait and think it over."

"I'm glad. Could I bother you with one more little detail?"

"What little detail?"

"Will you throw away the pills?"

"Well, I'll put them away."

"Would you mind doing it now?"

"Okay." She was gone for a few minutes, then returned. "See, I'll do whatever you say."

"How obliging. Thanks a lot. Really."

"Thank you. I'm sorry about calling you."

"I'm glad you did, if it helped."

The calls began to come more frequently—happy Saturday and

blue Monday calls. Brenda was supposed to audit a class on Monday afternoons, although she had finished taking all of the courses necessary, but she stopped going because she was worried that Andy would make a suicide call.

"Have you thought about maybe talking to a feminist therapist or something instead of calling me?" she would say. "I do like talking with you, but I am in Washington—just a trifle far. A therapist probably wouldn't cost much more than the phone bills."

"I don't think I want to talk to a shrink."

"I can understand that. I'm not too enthusiastic about them either. Of course, I wouldn't advise going to anybody but a feminist—maybe that would be different."

Brenda called some Washington feminist therapists, but none knew of any colleagues in Cleveland.

Brenda also tried to persuade Andy to give her a phone number. "I get so worried about you. Sometimes I wish I could call back just to find out how you're doing. I can't see why I shouldn't have your phone number."

"I guess I just don't trust you enough. Sure, you seem okay, great—but I don't want people knowing I'm gay. I don't like to have gay friends call me—at work or at home."

"For God's sake, what do you think I'm going to say, 'Hello, I'm Andy's gay friend'? How would anyone ever know?"

"I just want to be safe."

Not that Brenda was totally open. She didn't tell Andy about Ted until Andy started talking about coming to Washington and going to graduate school.

"Please do. You can stay with me, although I just have a one-bedroom apartment, a cat, and—you'll pardon the expression—a sort of husband. I haven't slept with him in over a year—not since I decided to be a lesbian. Please don't be too horrified." The words tumbled out quickly.

"You? You, of all people, have a husband? Well, well. Aren't you a surprise?"

"Are you going to tease me? I guess I have to suffer that. You aren't angry or disillusioned or anything? The truth is that I haven't even officially come out yet, though I know I love women. I got turned down by one lady. So I'm not a certified lesbian. I don't practice what I preach yet, but I will someday."

"My goodness! She doesn't have her lesbian's license yet! Why, I could sue you for giving advice without a license."

The next call was less cheery.

"Why shouldn't I take pills if I want to? Nobody would miss me."

"I would."

"That's nice of you to say, but I don't know if it's true. What have I ever done to help you? You have plenty of friends."

"A few, but I don't exactly enjoy losing them."

Brenda tried to go back to her books, although it was always hard after this kind of call. Marxism. That was her "specialty" because feminism supposedly wasn't a real political theory.

After spending much of the day studying in her apartment, she was restless. When Ted came in, she volunteered to go to the market so she could stretch her legs. Her volunteering to do such a chore was a most unusual event, and Ted quickly accepted.

She took her time, wandering on a few side streets to look for early signs of spring.

When she walked in the door, Ted hurried over to her.

"A friend of your friend Andy just called. She said Andy took some pills. She left a note saying to call you."

"No! Is she dead?"

"The woman was taking her to the hospital."

Brenda nearly lunged at him. "Did you get the woman's name? Or a phone number?"

"No."

"Damn, then I can't reach her. Andy—I was just talking to her this afternoon." She put down the bag of groceries, slumped into a chair, and covered her face with her hands.

"I thought I talked her out of it. I didn't. She took them. I failed and she took them."

"I'm sorry. You did all you could."

"No, I didn't. Or she wouldn't have taken them. She said she wouldn't. It's my fault."

"No, it isn't."

"How can I ever know it isn't? Oh, damnit, I'm not good enough to play god. Excuse me, I just want to be alone."

Brenda went to the other room.

Andy might die. I didn't say the right thing. If I'd said the right thing, maybe she wouldn't have done this.

How can you do that, damn you? How can you let your life depend on whether another person says the right thing? I don't want to have that kind of responsibility for anyone. What a fool I am, thinking that I'm the great life-giver.

4

In January, Brenda had joined a woman poets collective. At that point she wanted to join anything—anything besides *Womanpaper*. Nobody loved her or understood her, etc. Like an errant spouse, she wanted to wander to where she would feel more appreciated, but she would never, never leave *Womanpaper*. The newspaper had published some lesbian separatist papers and she fought over whether straight women could be feminist (she said they could).

Her first few months on the paper had brought evenings of talk, one trip to the Chesapeake Bay that *almost* worked, some good moments—but not enough. There was just one couple on the paper—Sky and Nicole—and everyone, struck as much by the glamour of their lesbianism as by the individual personalities, was drawn to them. When they broke up, everyone felt diminished, annoyed at having no one to bolster their illusions.

Nina was a fundamental friend, but Nina had just fallen in love with her first woman lover, Margo, and was about as accessible as the Queen of England. Once a month, Brenda was allocated a lunch or dinner with Nina and Margo—a strong-looking woman who had been a lesbian long enough not to expect everyone in the world to be one, who talked of ivy league schools, fencing, and crusading journalism. Behind Margo's occasional bluster was a fundamental decency and intelligence.

When Womenpoets began, Brenda joined nervously. She brought poems to read to the dozen women, crowded in an apartment. One after another, they read their poems. Their words moved her. She read hers, and, in turn, received acknowledgment that she could write poetry. Astounded, she wrote more poems for the group's next meeting.

Womenpoets quickly melted down to eight women. They met every other week, reading their poetry and planning dates for public readings. Sometimes they commented that a poem was weak, and Brenda trusted their judgment, which was frequently positive and almost always calm and reasonable.

The public readings made her feel as if she was living in another dimension, her true one. She couldn't have made an extemporaneous speech without quavering or trailing off, particularly if she had to answer questions, but she could put the whole force of her emotion into reading her poems. She felt as if she were a better self, herself crystallized, without hesitancy or embarrassment. That first night when they read at the Club Madame, a lesbian bar, she felt that she was showing her real self to the community for the first time. Several women from *Womanpaper* came to hear her, and she felt that she could speak to them more truly in poems than at meetings.

The poems had to show her love for women. About half of them that came to her were love poems. But she was terrified that women would learn about Ted and denounce her as a bisexual or hypocrite. She had made a conscious decision not to be actively bisexual, even in transition. She had not touched Ted for more than a year before she began giving poetry readings. But she felt unable to leave completely until a woman loved her. She read him her poetry and felt a little guilty that she would never allow him to hear her read in public. Against reason, she hoped that no woman would reject her because of his existence. Every time she read, she imagined a confrontation.

Miraculously, none ever happened. Either women did not know, or those who knew were kind, realizing that her lesbian poems represented her real self. She counted herself damn lucky.

When she returned home from a weekend in the country with Womenpoets, Andy called. When she heard Andy's voice, Brenda cried. "Oh, damnit, I thought I let you die. Oh, how are you?"

"I'm okay," weakly.

"Where are you?"

"The hospital."

"Did I say anything wrong in that last conversation? I've been so worried. Oh, please be all right."

"No, yes. Of course, you didn't say anything wrong. I'm sorry you thought that. After I talked with you, some folks from my office came by to see me and they made some cracks about gays. I joined them. I was a traitor. I hate myself when I'm a traitor. So I took some pills—figured I was no loss. But you know the kid—I came back—was in a coma for days, they say."

"You are all right, Andy?"

"Sure, I'm all right. More than I deserve to be, I guess."

"Don't say that! I can't tell you how horrible I felt when I thought you might be dead. I really like you. And I'm so frightened of having the responsibility of talking to you when you're feeling suicidal."

"I'm sorry. I guess you do get tired of me. If you want, I'll stop."

"No, not if you won't go to anyone else. I'm not tired of you. I'll read you a poem."

Morbid

In your dark nights
Come to me
I am the companion of sorrow
The suicide's best friend
I can listen endless hours, holding hands
Or coaxing disembodied voices
Across telephone wires
To hide away the pills.
If you want to die,
By all means tell me about it—
I'm the next step
Before the mortician.
Oh God, don't you see
What a fraud I am?
Listening, dispensing advice
Like a priest
Hidden in his stall
Knowing that although your storms may pass through me
While I shake
And sometimes leave a trail of debris
There are other moments
When I just observe your weather
And report it
In a sympathetic voice.
I do not always find the right tone
Sometimes I want your storm to cease
So I can eat dinner.
But I cannot let you know
Someone must seem to care
At your third suicide call
Or your twentieth

Who knows when you mean it?
Can't you see
That someone so involved
In deadly moments
Whose hand is pulling others'
From bottles of oblivion
Must have a lust for pilling
In her own head
And cares too much for sleep.
But nothing stops that nasty itch
To sleep
As much as the sight
Of a friend's coffin.
Yes, talk to me if you can
But life is so much better than I am.
Death is a sham like me
A false priest
Before an empty altar.
I don't want to sit
On the gravestones of my friends
Live, damn you, live.

"Wow! 'Live, damn you, live.' That's really something."

"I hope it isn't too harsh. I do get a little carried away. My poetry gets kind of dramatic."

"Oh, you are a fierce lady. I can't get over you writing a poem like that about me. Don't worry, I don't feel much like dying now, after all this time in the hospital. I want to live and get out of here."

"Good. I'm so glad you're okay."

A nurse came in and said something to Andy about getting off the phone.

When Brenda hung up the phone and walked back to the living room, Ted chided her for talking so long.

Brenda was enraged. "A woman recovering from a suicide attempt! Of course I talked to her! Of course that was ten times more important than talking to you! How could you possibly think otherwise?"

"I never see you anymore."

Unfortunately, she thought, that's not true.

"I don't mind Andy," he continued. "I mind everything."

"The feminist movement is the most important thing in my life. I've made that clear for a long time."

Andy called frequently that week.

"I've been thinking of moving to Washington," she said towards the end of the week. "I've always wanted to go there. That's why I subscribed to *Womanpaper*, to find out more about what's happening there."

"That's just fine. I'll finally get to meet you. You can stay with me, of course, if you want to. I hope my—pardon the expression—husband won't bother you. I'll find someplace else for you to stay if you want." Brenda gave her Nicole's number in case she wanted to stay in a place without a man.

"Great. I think I'm getting out of here today or tomorrow. I'd like to take a bus to D.C. tomorrow, if that's okay with you."

"Of course. We're giving another poetry reading tonight. It's vain of me, but I wish you were going to be here."

"To hear you read? I wish I were, too. Well, I'll hear you someday. Will you read the poem about me?"

"You wouldn't mind?"

"Mind? No, I'd like it."

Of course she wanted the reading to last forever; there was a letdown afterwards, as usual. Going home was always hard, crowded into a car of newspaper women, trying to pretend not to be totally absorbed in the fact that she had just been part of the poetry reading. She told about Andy's coming and they warned her that Andy might not be such a great person. One acquaintance tried to tell her that Andy was probably dangerous or crazy and that she was out of her mind to take her in. Brenda was annoyed, but of course she was afraid. She had no idea what Andy was really like, or not enough idea. What if she was tough? Was she middle-class, or from the ghetto? What if she tried to kill herself while she was in D.C.? Brenda got the number of a feminist therapist from Nina.

Fortunately, Ted hadn't been too surprised when Brenda asked if Andy could stay with them. "You've already asked her, haven't you," he said indulgently. Of course she had—of course she always would.

Shortly after she returned home, Nicole called. "I didn't want to tell you earlier and spoil your evening, but just before I left for the poetry reading, your friend Andy called me. She was screaming something about being moved somewhere. I tried to get her to tell me where she was, or give me a number, but she got off the phone —or was pulled away from it. I don't know what happened."

"Oh, my God. Isn't there any more? Didn't she say anything else?"

"She said to tell you she was being taken away. That's all."

"Nothing else? How will I find her? Oh, damn, I guess I'll call all of the hospitals in Cleveland and ask if they have her. Oh God, I don't know her last name. The damn woman hasn't told me her name. Oh, why in hell didn't she?"

She soon got off the phone and called Cleveland information, asking for numbers of all the hospitals in town. Oh Jesus, she kept saying, there I was on a damn stage reading my poetry and something had happened to Andy and I didn't even know it.

Brenda called each hospital, asking, "Pardon me, but do you have a young black woman patient named Andy—that may not be her legal name—whom you admitted last week for attempted suicide? I'm trying to locate her."

Most of the people who spoke to her were rude and incredulous. "What are you talking about, lady?" "What's her name?" "I don't know what her name is." "Well, how do you expect us to know something about someone whose name you don't know?" All of them said they had no such patient. By the time she had called the last hospital, she gave up. There was nothing left to do, but she kept feeling that there must be something she could and should do. She had a wild impulse to go to Cleveland, but what could be more ridiculous than going to a strange city to look for a woman whose name you didn't know, when you didn't know what she looked like.

For the next day or so, Brenda hung around the phone, but there was no word from Andy. People who had been told that she was coming heard the story skeptically; most of them said, "told you she's a little weird," and those who refrained from saying it seemed to think it.

As the weeks went by, Brenda began feeling somewhat resentful of Andy, unsure that anything could really be keeping her incommunicado and annoyed at never having been told her real name.

5

Brenda took her exam and passed. The thought of leaving Ted was terrifying. What would it be to live again without someone who knew and cared what you ate for dinner? Who was always willing to walk down the street beside you, so you didn't have to go alone? Would she ever have gone to those evening seminars on Chinese politics at George Washington University if Ted hadn't come there to go home with her? Not to mention her late night classes at Catholic University, over in northeast Washington—how much she had wanted him then. Another human presence—she needed another human presence in her life, nearby.

It must be a woman's presence—she had learned that. Standing beside him, she longed for a woman. What if this was just the inevitable isolation one meets in trying to be close to another person—perhaps it would be no different with a woman, perhaps she would still seek some other presence.

And if there was no woman? Would she risk the void for the sake of an imaginary woman, a possible woman? Were the word "lesbian," magic though it was, and a blank space beside her enough to give up Ted?

With Ted, free from the fear of being alone, an atom lost in some possibly sordid world, she had written more, accomplished more than at any previous time of her life. She was afraid of losing that stability which permitted work. Unlike many of her contemporaries, she was not contemptuous of stability—she loved it.

Nervously, she went before the *Womanpaper* meeting. Not

looking at anyone, she responded to the question, "Does anybody want the office job?"

"I'd like it, if that's all right with everybody. I've made up my mind to leave Ted, but I'm afraid to do it without any money. I love the office—I want to work there. And he'll let me save all of my salary" (fifty dollars a week) "so I can leave. Maybe I'll have enough by January, when I'll have finished my exams. Is that all right?" Most people on the collective were not supported by husbands—many lived on less money than she and Ted did. She was nervous about the response, but everyone either said, "that's fine," or said nothing.

"You're sure it's all right, even though I'm going to save the money? I don't want anyone to mind later."

"It's all right," said one woman, not a close friend, slightly impatiently. Margo, a somewhat friendly presence, said briskly, "That's settled; let's move on."

"Thank you, thank you so much. This means a lot."

She felt ambivalent about the group. Small groups were the hope and the danger of the movement. The hope, because they seemed to be the only way to democratic communication and non-hierarchical decision making. The danger, because the members brought out one another's weaknesses—cruelty, cowardice, desire to be part of the latest fashion, dominance, passive aggression—the list was becoming obvious. They also provided a chance to be a fully functioning political individual rather than part of a mass.

None of them really knew how to use these groups, how to handle themselves within these groups. They were constantly feeling guilty about missed opportunities or unkind impulses. It is hard enough to learn how to interact well with another person, but with a whole group—incredibly complex. To achieve a good, well-working feminist collective was the equivalent of strangers meeting and dancing in a harmonious, coordinated ballet, with no choreographer.

The terrifying thing about the women's movement, as Brenda observed to another collective member one day, was that it showed you, unmistakably, that life was just made up as you go along. If you stayed in more established work, such as law, you might be able to continue believing that everything went according to prearranged rules, that somebody knew clearly what she was doing and what the results would be.

Restless, she patrolled the spring, seizing upon each violet as if it was a personal affront because she could not share it with a lover. Ted was always urging her to take weekend walks. Sometimes she assented, strolling with him down through the strip of green Rock Creek Park that curls down beyond the Shoreham Hotel and leads by a meager woods toward Georgetown. Small beds of daffodils, cunningly interspersed along the parkway by the National Park Service, annoyed her because Ted's eyes saw them. She could not flirt; she barely smiled. Some woman must come and take her away from all this. Resenting him, she was grateful for his presence. Walking alone through spring flowers would be a provocation to tears. She did not want to be lost, to float away, unnoticed, unspoken to. A person wanted to walk beside her, accepted her choice of restaurant for dinner. If there were no weekends, would husbands be necessary?

Other weekends, his mere presence was more than she could stand. A person was necessary, but it must—yes, must—be a woman. She dashed to the *Womanpaper* office, hoping to find one of the collective members there, and crying when she didn't.

There must be a woman somewhere who would love her. Well, no, there didn't have to be but she hoped.

Brenda had a very brief affair with a friend who broke it off the first time she saw Brenda cry, on the grounds that Brenda was too emotional!

Brenda's attitude could have been summed up in the words, "Is that all there is?" There must be something more to lesbian love than this, or why leave Ted—at least she could occasionally express a feeling around him. She wasn't heartbroken, but she felt she should have been heartbroken—these things should matter more. A word or two should not be enough to finish them.

After all, as she told one of her friends, she didn't become a lesbian because she wanted to avoid feelings, but because she wanted to express them.

Her life seemed solitary—at such moments she felt that Ted was gone already and no one else would ever share her life. Lesbianism wasn't really going to be an alternative—no woman would ever love her. Maybe she didn't have the kind of personality that women loved.

Andy moved against the straps, as if some effort on her part could break them. Drugs slowed her movements, but nothing about her was subdued. Muscled white men in white coats impassively restrained her struggling.

"Fight back, fight back, it's your own fault if you don't fight back," she told herself. "Damned fool, you would get yourself here." "You bastards," she screamed.

A picture of a naked woman, blonde, looking like somebody's centerfold, was flashed in front of her.

Lightning pain shook her.

"No! No!" she felt herself screaming. So that was what an electric shock felt like. It was over. Would they do it again?

Another picture. Another shock.

I'll die. I can't stand it.

The doctor, a big, middle-aged white man with glasses, leaned toward her. "Dirty dyke. Filthy nigger dyke. You won't be a dyke anymore, will you?"

Her voice got forced out somehow. "Yes, yes I will."

He jolted her.

I'll die. No, he can't do that. Get it together. Live, damn you, live. Yeah, life. Yeah, I'm gay.

He just kept doing it.

6

After every issue of *Womanpaper* was printed, there followed a post-mortem at which the collective discussed each article and its layout on the page. Not infrequently, there was outrage at a sentence — or a whole article — because someone disagreed with the politics expressed.

This issue contained an article telling lesbians in the military how to avoid dishonorable discharges, and Brenda had heard some women muttering that it was politically incorrect to help anyone remain within the military. She was eager to hear the discussion.

Just as the post-mortem began, the phone in the next room rang and someone said it was for Brenda. Grumbling, sure that it was Ted trying to make his loneliness known as usual (why on earth he couldn't make friends or join organizations connected with his own interests—such as mountaineering—she couldn't see), she picked it up and none too graciously helloed.

"Hello. This is me. Andy."

"Andy. Well, it's certainly been a long time. What on earth happened to you? I almost gave up on you."

"Oh, plenty of things have happened. You don't sound very sympathetic." Her voice was strange.

"I am glad to hear from you, really. Are you out of the hospital?"

"Yes, I'm out *now*."

"Andy, there's a *Womanpaper* meeting going on in the other room and I wonder if you could call back in a few hours, after I get home." After waiting all these weeks, she doesn't have to talk to me in the middle of a meeting. In the two years since she had joined the collective, Brenda had missed only three meetings, all when she was out of town, and she had always called long distance to learn what was happening.

"Call back! That's all it matters to you! No, I won't call back. Not ever." Andy was furious, speaking in a voice Brenda had never heard before.

"Oh, for heaven's sake, I didn't mean to upset you. I'm sorry. I'll talk now if you want. I just happen to care about meetings."

"More than you care about me. I know my place. Go back to your meeting. Good-bye." She hung up.

For God's sake. Did she think Brenda had nothing else to do in the world but wait for her calls? Well, it was a long wait. But upsetting Andy felt horrible, really horrible. What could have happened to her? What would she do now? Maybe she needed Brenda, and Brenda had forfeited her chance to help.

Two days later, Brenda was sitting alone in the office, entering subscription checks into the books. The phone rang.

"Hello. Do you want to talk to me *now*?" Andy's voice was much calmer but still not its usual pitch.

"Of course I do. I'm so sorry. I didn't mean to offend you."

"You did. I almost didn't call back."

"Don't think I haven't been worried. I was. What happened to you?"

Andy's voice was breaking slightly. "They took me to the psychiatric ward. They kept me there, tied up. They were pretty rough."

"Oh my God! Oh Andy, Andy, I'm so sorry. Did they hurt you very much?"

"Pretty much. They gave me electric shocks."

"Andy! Andy. Oh, they didn't dare. How are you?" Suddenly she felt closer to the horrors of this world than ever before. They did not just happen to women in articles in feminist publications. They happened to people you knew.

"Oh, I guess I'll be okay." Andy's tone was warmer. "For awhile there I wasn't so sure. But you know me, I live through anything."

"Thank God you do! Oh, Andy, I wish I could have stopped it! I did call every hospital in Cleveland. But all I could do was ask whether they had a young black woman who had tried to commit suicide—I didn't even know your name."

"That's true, you didn't. You really called all those places? Yes, you would." (Softly) "I'll bet they wouldn't have told you the truth even if you did know my name."

"Won't you tell me your name now? I've been so frustrated about not having it."

"Soon—I will soon."

"Honestly, sometimes I think you're Patricia Hearst or somebody, you're so mysterious."

"Not hardly." Andy let her voice be mildly humorous. "I'm so glad to talk to you. It's really been bad. The pain was—it wasn't too cool—and they kept trying to make me say I'd stop being a lesbian, but I wouldn't."

"Andy. You are brave."

"I didn't feel brave. I was scared. I didn't know if I'd ever get out. I kept remembering that line of yours, 'live, damn you, live.'I kept thinking about you, thinking there was somebody who'd be glad when I got out, somebody who'd understand what I'd been through. And then I called you, and you didn't want to talk to me."

"Andy, Andy, if I'd had the least idea! I'm sorry. I didn't know. I'll never, never do that again."

"I'll never call you during a meeting again."

"Oh, the meeting doesn't matter."

"Uh huh. I was so disgusted I almost didn't call back."

"I'm glad you did."

"So am I." The voice was warmer again.

"When did you get out?"

"A few days ago. Somebody working at the hospital got sorry for me and helped me get out."

"So you weren't discharged?"

"No. I keep wondering what if somebody wants to get me back there. This time, I'll fight if anybody tries."

"God, I hope they don't want to get you back. Be careful."

"You bet I'm careful."

"Does your family know?"

"Are you kidding? All they know is that I was missing for a couple of weeks—I sometimes go away like that. They don't know about the suicide. My friends try not to tell them about my suicide attempts."

"You don't think the hospital was in touch with them?"

"No, they don't know a thing."

Awful questions about the family entered Brenda's mind, but she didn't convey them.

Being an office worker for *Womanpaper* made Brenda feel

almost like one of the real workforce whose ranks she had rarely joined. There were no specified hours, but she tried to rise early enough to arrive at work during the morning. She was in the work-world, but not of it. She joked that jeans were her uniform (if it had been left up to her to choose movement fashions, she might have selected others), plus t-shirt or turtleneck. Her blue tennis shoes were beginning to get holes in the toes. Her watch, however, had cost about sixty dollars. She was not comfortable with Timexes—a Timex would make her feel poorer than holes in her shoes. She wanted a wide band and large face, but not a *grossly* large face. All of her life she had nice watches, and she wanted to continue, though aware of the incongruity. Her purse, a large, beflowered carpetbag, even after carpetbags went out of style, was a link to the texture of past ages. It always contained at least five pounds of papers, books, hairbrushes, keys, and Coke cans.

She was always pleased to open the office door and find herself alone—although lately, she had started wishing for her co-worker Dolly's presence. Plopping down on an old chair with half its stuffing out, a chair that should have swiveled but lurched instead, she could feel that she was one with the paper, close to its heartbeat. The peeling brown walls with long-forgotten posters were just the right shade to feel properly radical.

She dragged out the ledger and started entering six-dollar sub-scription checks and writing down the subscribers' addresses on the proper forms. Brenda had avoided clerical work for other or-ganizations, but this was different. Each one of these women would read the articles in the paper, would at moments see those parts of Brenda's soul that were revealed in her words. She would never know them as well as they might know her—frustrating. She tried to glean as much information as she could from the name, the ad-dress, the stationery, the occasional note enclosed. It was exciting to recognize the names, seen before, of the old subscribers, renew-ing.

One of the best things about the office job was the other office worker, Dolly Duncan.

Like most of the other women on the collective, Brenda had been skeptical when a woman named Dolly Duncan wanted to join the paper. I mean, it's pretty nervy for a radical feminist to have a name like Dolly Duncan, to look like Daisy Mae, *and* to have a chirpy voice that always sounded ready to burst into singing. People thought she was straight—and she was straight. Dolly was considered minimally acceptable because a woman of properly dykish appearance always swore that she was going to bring Dolly out. Dolly worked long and hard hours for the paper and the other woman only made an occasional appearance to say she felt guilty about doing so little work, but there was no doubt who was considered more "correct."

Dolly's other problem—as if her appearance wasn't problem enough—was that she had started out by saying that she wanted everyone to be nice to each other, "give strokes." At the moment, that was the least fashionable thing she could have said—Dolly frequently said the least fashionable thing, often unwittingly.

Brenda had known from the beginning that she and Dolly would be friends, but refrained from being friendly for quite a while because she was tired of befriending the undergoats and scapedogs, which seemed her inevitable role.

They had both wanted the office job, and Dolly had claimed her loyalty by saying, "You take it. You want it more."

"No, no, don't just give up like that."

"It's all right—I'm on unemployment. I can do it for a while without getting paid."

So Dolly began working on the office job without pay, and became an official worker soon when the next vacancy was available.

Brenda and Dolly worked well together, and talked at great length. Both wanted a renewal of the time of demonstrations and marches.

Unless something unusual happened, receiving the mail was the highlight of the day. Brenda would go downstairs again and again, eager to see whether it had arrived. Then she would carry it up, tumble it on her desk, and pry through it. Anything that looked like a letter to the editor was read first, then mail from subscription agencies, which might include large checks for library accounts, then what appeared to be regular subscriptions.

Brenda particularly enjoyed seeing that readers were requesting back issues. She was a back issues fetishist—had spent an entire year indexing every article in old issues, going back to 1970, hoping to earn vast sums for the paper from the sale of the index.

Some back issues were in demand—those that had reported on particularly explosive movement controversies or had contained a number of articles about love.

Today there was a letter that asked for a *full set* of back issues, from 1970 on—and from an individual reader, not a library. Someone cared! A woman really wanted to read through their history. Her name was Karen Carpenter and her return address was a town named Fenwick, with a zip code that was similar to the code for Cleveland.

It was Andy, of course. She smiled, certain, and quickly packaged bundles of newspapers to send her.

Later Andy called.

"Karen Carpenter, I presume," said Brenda, hoping that she was as smart as she thought she was.

"How'd you know? Genius, I knew you'd guess." Andy sounded pleased.

"Elementary, my dear Andy. You live near Cleveland. In Fenwick—on the postmark of your suicide letter. You suddenly showed a great interest in the paper. Who else?"

"Well, now that you have my name and address, smart one, you might as well have my phone numbers, too. But it's better to call me at work than at home. I have trouble talking free sometimes because of my grandmother."

They felt closer after that day—although it was impossible to think of Andy as anybody but Andy.

The telephone rang in the other room and Brenda rushed off to answer it, bumping into several pieces of furniture on the way.

"Hello."

"Want to hear some gloomy news, or are you sick of it by now? Seems like that's all I have."

"Tell me, please."

"I went to a doctor today—she was a pretty nice doctor, I guess."

"A woman doctor. That's nice."

"You bet a woman doctor. I'm not letting any more men get their hands on me. They've done their thing already. This woman doctor told me that the shock treatments have given me a blood clot in the head."

"Oh, my God! In the head! How bad is it?"

"It's bad enough. Maybe I'll live."

"Andy! Only maybe?"

"Yeah, she wasn't sure what the percentages are. They're trying to decide whether they ought to operate."

"Andy. It can't be. Is there anything I can do?"

"I don't know. Isn't it crazy? I want to live now. All that time in the hospital, I knew I wanted to live. I didn't want them to get me. But it looks like the bastard got to me anyway."

"At least you have the will now. They haven't done you in yet."

"I wish I could get that bastard. I'd like to take a gun, go to the hospital, and wait 'til he came out."

"No, no, don't make the bastard a martyr. He isn't worth risking your life for."

"At least he couldn't do it to anybody else."

"They'll say that you were crazy and make him into some kind of martyr. You don't want that, do you?"

"No, but I wouldn't mind getting back at him."

"To hell with him. You're more important than he is. The best way for you to vanquish him is to survive and refuse to let him destroy your life. Please try to survive. If you think you have a good doctor now, try to work with her and take care of yourself. I've never even had a chance to meet you. You can't die before we've met, okay?"

Brenda thought about going to Cleveland if Andy was going to have an operation. She was suddenly overcome with the poignancy of never seeing Andy's face. She wanted Andy to become a friend — Andy was a friend — and pictured them knowing each other for years, laughing back at the days of suicide calls. Brenda actually called the airlines, train and bus stations to find out how much it cost to go to Cleveland. Of course, it would be silly to see Andy just briefly, if she were going to go into the hospital and have an operation, but Brenda found that she wanted that very much.

However, the doctor decided to use anti-coagulant drugs instead, so Brenda's urgency about a trip relaxed. But she had got the idea into her head and wasn't going to forget it completely.

Andy insisted she wasn't ready for it yet.

Brenda tried to discuss Andy's shock treatments and blood clot with her friends, but they resisted. Some simply wouldn't listen. Her old annoyance over the suicide note was revived. Made of stone, that's what they were.

7

Brenda had written Andy a letter telling about her life, because she was a writer and wanted to show that side of herself.

Brenda dragged herself to a mailbox, opened it with a little key, and found a wonderfully fat scented envelope, white-pink, postmarked from the Cleveland post box.

There were many numbered pages of stationery and three pictures.

The pictures showed a brown woman with large eyes. The eyes and face muscles tried to smile but there were signs of stress. The face looked gentle, warm, vulnerable; it was the face of a woman whose heart had been broken. Short, silky, curly black hair framed her. She sat in a white living room with a beamed ceiling, on a dark green sofa with cushions that had petit point red roses on them.

Brenda's mother also had a white living room with a beamed ceiling, and a dark green couch with cushions covered with petit point red roses.

Dear Brenda,

How can I thank you for all you've done for me. I loved your letter telling me all about yourself—you are truly a wonderful woman. I don't talk much about my life, but I want to tell you about it now.

My father died when I was a baby and my mother left me to be raised by my grandparents. They were very good to me.

I had cerebral palsy and had to spend years in bed. My legs are small and I am very short (4'10") because of that. But people were good to me. I had warm, sweet nurses. That's how I began to love women.

I went to a small, religious college and majored in pre-social work. Even though some of the courses were kind of strange and some of the teachers were funny about blacks, I liked it because I thought it would help me to do somebody some good.

My college roommate was very pretty and I loved her. Somehow we got together and I was happy. At the end of my sophomore year she told me that she was going to get married! She had told me that there was no one else, but she had been engaged all of the time and saw him on the weekends when she went home. I couldn't stand it. That was the first time I tried to kill myself. I didn't succeed at that, but I wouldn't go back to college. I didn't want to see her with him.

Sometimes I tried to date men and go straight, but I couldn't. There were a couple of nice guys—Bob, later Al—who wanted to marry me, but I couldn't force myself to sleep with them. I knew that wasn't right for me.

My grandfather died, and I ran his shop for a while. He was kind to me—losing him really hurt.

My old desire to help people came out again and I got a job for a neighborhood center and started taking courses in paralegal work. I spent a lot of time in the neighborhood downtown.

One of the extension courses I took at the university was a course on poverty law taught by this really sympathetic older woman professor. She was white, but she didn't ever put people down. She really cared. I was just crazy about her. I'd sit in class, staring at her every minute.

One day she asked me to come to her home to talk about the class. I was so nervous that I had a hard time getting there, but I couldn't stay away either. She served me coffee and cake and was talking so nice and we were so close that I just burst into tears. She went down beside me and made love to me, and it was the most beautiful experience I ever had. I was in heaven—I couldn't believe it. I couldn't do anything but cry.

Her name was Maxy. We were lovers from then on, for the next five years. I moved in with her and we had a wonderful life. We went to movies, concerts, and museums together. We tried to help people whenever we could—she was so generous. Nobody else has ever been so kind to me. I loved her with all my heart and she loved me too.

4:30 a.m. Sunday

One day last spring Maxy was hit by a car while she was crossing a street. The dude who did it was drunk. I just got to the hospital in time to see her die. She was so brave, trying to calm me down. I wish I could have died instead. I never felt so horrible. I screamed and sobbed. The hospital was so cold. Nobody cared what was happening to her.

I've missed her so much. Our home belongs to her family and they are selling it. I went back to live with my grandmother. My family knew that Maxy was a good friend of mine but I've had to hide how much she meant. I only have a couple of gay friends. It felt like everything was gone when Maxy died. I think I'm always going to be celibate — I haven't had any interest in anyone since she died.

I've spent a lot of time on my work. Some of the people we try to help really need it. So I try to tell myself that's important, that's enough for me. But I get very depressed sometimes—and I guess you know the rest.

Maybe I just need to get away. Maybe I should move to Washington or somewhere. Here, I keep thinking about her. And I keep thinking about what happened to me in the hospital and I get frightened that it's going to happen to me again, they're going to get me back.

5 p.m. Sunday

I can't believe how much I've told you. Some of these things I've never told anyone before. I'm used to hiding a lot. I can't believe anybody really wants to listen to me. You're so sympathetic.

I think you're a really fine person. Maybe I don't have any right to say it, but I think that woman who was your lover was crazy not to appreciate you. You'll meet somebody fine—you deserve it. Don't worry about what people think about your husband. Anybody can see you're sincere. I was so glad that you took the time to write me that long letter about your life. I've spent all weekend writing you this letter about mine.

I enclosed some pictures of the kid so you could see what I look like. They were taken last week when some relatives came over to my grandmother's house. It was my 27th birthday. I still look pretty shaky from the time in the hospital, I guess.

I hope you don't mind reading such a long letter.

Very sincerely,
Andy

She touched the letter, looked at the photographs again, and reread it, committing every detail to memory. For the first time, she thought that perhaps Andy and she had many things in common. Serious. Monogamous. Sensitive. And the woman she had loved had been a Ph.D. and white, so those things were no barrier. And she likes me, Brenda thought.

But this is a breach of trust. What right do I have to become interested in somebody I've played therapist with? That sounds bad, like using her. How could it ever work? But Maxy was her teacher—isn't it similar? Andy didn't mind that. Andy has such a warm voice. Only a good person could write a letter like this. Sounds more open and sincere than plenty of feminists. So dark—so pretty. I shouldn't care about looks. What does it matter if someone is dark—but it does. Why? Is it because my mom used to have black hair? Why couldn't I be black Irish like the rest of the family. Oh, Brenda, you're so damn attracted to black people that you're racist. Better remember Sam. Don't want anything like that again, do you? Dumbest thing you ever did. Telling yourself you shouldn't go to grad school because he hadn't been to college. Pretending to be Lady Chatterley and worship his penis. What bullshit. But she sounds so sweet. She's a woman—that's different. Nobody else is that open. Hell, nobody is even monogamous. And she's seen my good side—maybe she knew that part of me better than anybody else. Maybe I'm better in a crisis than I am day-to-day. I don't show off well. She does like me, I think. Maybe a lot. Do I have any right to get involved with her? She wasn't thinking about that when she told me about her life. She stayed with Maxy five years—that's a long time. Poor Andy has been hurt so much—maybe I could make her feel better. I'm certainly being arrogant—why should she be attracted to me just because of the phone calls. That's a reason to be my friend, not my lover. What the hell am I thinking of anyway — she might die from the damn blood clot. Oh, no, she can't, please. I've got to know her—I've just got to know her.

She was sorry that she had to wait until morning to call Andy at work.

"Hello. This is Brenda. Thank you for the wonderful letter," was the first thing she said.

"Did you really think it was wonderful? You didn't mind that it was long?"

"You've actually had what I want—a long, good relationship with a woman. You've been a lesbian for so many years, seen so many sides of it, that I feel really strange about having lectured you about the importance of keeping faith in lesbianism—considering that I've had so little experience myself. Isn't that weird?"

"Maybe a little. But I think you understand what it's all about anyway."

"Thanks, I hope so. But you're the one who really knows what it is to be lesbian—who has lived the good part—and been forced to suffer for your lesbianism."

"I guess that's true. But I keep thinking about what happened to me. I can't forget. I don't know if any lesbian would ever want to touch me again." Her voice started cracking.

She's been raped. Of course that's it. She feels guilty about it, as if she were to blame. How can I let her know she isn't?

Brenda searched for words, quickly. "I'm sure you've been through many dreadful things, but I'm sure that any lesbian would respect that and try to be supportive."

"You don't know what happened."

"Maybe I do. I'm good at guessing."

"You're so smart. But I don't think I can tell you this—but I can't ever face you if I haven't told you."

"Why don't you try telling me, then. I haven't rejected you much so far, have I?"

"No, but this is different. I can't tell about it. Maybe I can write it."

"Then do, if you want to. I'm more than willing to know."

"I guess I will then. I would like to see you someday, but I want you to know this first."

Andy's letter arrived—special delivered by a messenger man in blue.

Much shorter than the earlier letter, it said,

Dear Brenda,

I don't know how to tell you this, but other bad things happened to me besides the shocks.

The doctor raped me, mostly up my anus. I am cut up there, and my (woman) doctor had to take lots of stitches.

He was so full of hate—he called me "nigger," "dyke," "whore," and lots of other names.

He hurt so much, I wanted to die. No, I wanted to get away, to kill him—anything.

No man ever had me before. This was so ugly—would any lesbian be able to touch me after this? Am I still a true lesbian?

Since I've been in the hospital I've been in so much misery that I can't even cry. I'm afraid they've wrecked me forever.

I don't think I could tell anybody else about this. What do you think?

Love
Andy

Brenda cried and ran to the phone immediately, while she was still crying. It was late in the afternoon, but Andy might still be at work.

"Andy?"

The voice was very hesitant. "Oh, hi. Did you get the letter?"

"Yes. Oh Andy, I'm sure no lesbian would ever turn away from you because of this. It could happen to any of us—any of us. I know other lesbians who've been raped. We're all oppressed—that's how they try to keep women down. It's not your fault. You shouldn't feel ashamed."

Andy could hardly talk. "You think so."

"I know so. It could happen to me tomorrow—would you say I wasn't a proper lesbian if it did?"

"No."

"Then don't feel that way about yourself. We mustn't let them divide us. We need each other."

"I guess so."

"The part about not crying really worried me. Do let yourself cry, if you want to."

"I'm afraid. Sometimes I think that maybe I could cry if I was with you."

"Do you want me to visit? Of course I will. We can just sit together and have a good cry about the terrible things they do. I can come to Cleveland this weekend, if you want. It's Friday afternoon, so I can just get on the bus and . . ."

"No, no. Wait a minute. I don't know if I can handle that. I'll have to think about it."

"Think and say yes."

"I don't know if I'm ready—I'll call you Saturday morning, okay?"

"Okay."

Brenda called the Greyhound station and memorized the Saturday bus schedule for Cleveland. She cashed a check at the bank and packed her black briefcase—inherited from Ted—with some extra socks, panties, and an extra banlon turtleneck. She told Ted that she might go to Cleveland that weekend to see Andy. Ted had been impressed with the sensitive face in the photograph.

About nine o'clock Saturday morning—when Ted was already out on his morning hike on the "C and O" canal—Andy called.

"You certainly are sympathetic. I am tempted to ask you to Cleveland."

"So ask me. What's the worst thing that could happen? You'll cry a little, I'll cry a little. Is that so terrible?"

"No, that doesn't sound too terrible. Maybe it would be a good idea."

"Of course it is. I'll take the 10:30 bus and be in Cleveland at 9:25. I hope you'll meet me at the station. I'll be wearing blue jeans and a jean jacket."

"Of course I'll meet you. The 10:30 bus. My goodness, you certainly are eager."

"Yes. And you can't change your mind. See you later—I've got to get ready."

Brenda hung up, worried that Andy would change her mind if she talked for too long. She got dressed and bustled off on her way, determined not to hear of any changes.

I am a knight on a charger, I am young Lochinvar, she kept telling herself. A feminist knight of course. How feminist is it to want to be a knight riding off to a damsel in distress? Not very. I hope she sees me as glamorous. Nobody sees me as glamorous, sees the part of me that is like a knight riding off on a charger.

They tortured and raped her, my Andy. My voice, Andy. How

could he? I can't stop thinking of the "Stabat Mater," remember singing it at the station of the cross every Lent.

> Bruised, derided, cursed, defiled.
> She beheld her tender child.
> All with bloody scourges rent.

Maybe I shouldn't see you like this—want to help, hold, soothe. Am I too arrogant? Why should I be the Virgin Mary—me? They did it—they did it to my Andy. They hurt her. I have to make it up to her, somehow. Andy I know, have talked to on the phone for months, Andy who told me her life story, Andy who was betrayed by her college lover, Andy who lived with Maxy, Andy who tried to kill herself—and Andy who calls me—they have hurt Andy. A man dared to rape Andy. Why, why, how could he? And she feels contaminated, poor brave Andy, Andy who survived the torture. They dared to hurt my friend. Bruised, derided, cursed, defiled . . . she wants me to help her, me, I have been called. Oh, Brenda Anne, you crazy damn fanatic, you. Knight, pieta, whatever—I'll be anything she needs.

Am I going to make love with her? I don't know. Is it right? Is it taking advantage? Why am I so excited? Just to be important to somebody, to matter—to show how much I can give—not to have to hold back in little affairs in which people never say, "I love you."

She took the "L" bus to downtown Washington, and walked a few blocks to the Greyhound station. The blocks were poor, mostly warehouses. Only a few men were on the streets—none said anything to her today.

The station was dingy. A long line of people was guided around posts and ropes to seedy-looking ticket windows. A few rows of salmon plastic chairs provided places for waiting passengers to sit.

The poor travel by bus. The difference between a bus station and an airport is staggering, and Brenda was more used to airports. She felt she did not know black and/or working class men well enough to know at a glance who was safe, who wasn't. She thought she could make fairly good guesses, but wasn't sure. These men smoked cigars, carried transistors. A few looked as if they might be winos or on drugs, hanging around the station. She was sorry for women who had to be around the winos, the men on drugs. Sorrier for them than the men themselves? Yes—she could more easily see herself having such men as fathers or brothers, than as being one of them. Or the others, who weren't on any chemicals, who were okay, but might not read books, might have been to a school system so bad that they never learned to read. So horrible. And did they face the horror, or accept it? Did she do any good by being a revolutionary, she who had never lived this horror? How good a revolutionary was she, how much would she give up? Never her books, never. She clutched the Elizabeth Bowen novel that she had brought to read on the bus.

Andy. Andy. Why is meeting her so exciting? Because of having the chance to play noble comforter? Maybe it won't work at all—-perhaps we'll just feel awkward in person, won't have anything to say to one another. But I don't believe that. Maybe I'm egotistical to go and see her like this, to presume that I can help, but I'm sure I'd be a worse person if I *didn't* want to.

What if she isn't there, what if we don't recognize each other—4'10" is small, though—there can't be too many four-foot ten-inch black lesbians in the bus station.

Cleveland itself loomed darkly—it seemed to be all towering factories.

Brenda walked into the station—it was much older, larger, and more crowded than the one in D.C. She'd never find Andy. She walked the length of the station, looking tentatively at each young-ish black woman she saw. My God, Andy *wasn't* there. She wanted to panic. Some Lochinvar. Stupid. What if something happened to Andy? She walked back through the station again, searching the women's faces, even those she had seen before. Certainly none seemed very pleased by her inquiring glance.

She saw a woman sitting in a plastic chair. The woman suddenly stood up and walked over to her, saying softly, "Are you Brenda Anne Dougherty?"

"Yes. Andy?"

"That's me. Hello."

They smiled at each other, flushing, blushing, or some equivalent thereof.

Andy was small—the top of her head reached just above Brenda's breasts, and Brenda was not astoundingly tall, only 5'7". Although Andy was plump, there was something delicate about her—her features were so small. But there was also something strong, suggesting a command of herself—Brenda had the impression that Andy was about forty, although her face was obviously much younger. She wore a pale blue pantsuit—her appearance somehow suggested a "no-nonsense" working woman and yet—pardon the word—was "feminine." Her smile was small, but you believed it meant something.

"I was so afraid that I wouldn't find you. I didn't see you."

"Did you think I'd leave *you* waiting at the station. No way."

"I didn't really think that, but I was worried anyway."

"Let me take your bag."

"No, of course not, it's nothing."

"Let me get you some dinner—the cafeteria here isn't so great, but it'll do."

"Thank you." She didn't want to admit she had already eaten, in case Andy was hungry.

They walked toward the cafeteria together. They were the most conspicuous pair in the place—people looked at the tallish, pale white woman and the small black woman, walking as if they belonged together. Brenda felt that they did belong together.

They both bought chicken sandwiches and Cokes and sat at a table. "I'm a Coca-Cola addict. I have to have it to wake up in the morning. Is there somewhere around here where we can find a pack?"

"I got us a room at the Holiday Inn. They have Coke machines on all floors. So you're a coca-holic too?" They smiled at one another.

"Definitely. I drink about four a day."

"Me too."

"At last I'm here."

"You sure are. I couldn't believe how fast you said you'd take the 10:30 bus—and how fast you got off the phone." She chuckled.

"I was afraid you'd change your mind and tell me not to come."

"Oh, I would have if you'd given me a chance. I tried to call back, but you had already gone."

"Isn't it just as well this way?"

"Oh, you're right as usual, I guess."

The smiles and eye exchanges were so warm that Brenda felt she must be blushing constantly. Talking with other women wasn't this intimate. Every least word felt like a particular event in getting to know one another.

"You're not finishing your sandwich," Andy chided.

"I'm too full. I ate dinner at the stopover—I just didn't want to be rude or stop you from having dinner."

"I've already had dinner, too. Waiting has been so hard."

They laughed and put aside the rest of their sandwiches.

Andy called a cab to take them to the Holiday Inn. The city was forbidding, very grim compared with Washington.

The cab left them at the entrance to a large hotel. The extraordinarily heavy glass doors led them into a green-carpeted, palm-treed lobby that was more elaborate than Brenda had expected from the familiar old name. Her family had taken her to many hotels when she was growing up, but she had not been to many since she acquired a social conscience and blue jeans.

Aware of her scruffiness, she didn't know whether she was more bothered by the large holes in the toes of her tennis shoes or the braided uniforms the employees had to wear.

Andy steered her to the registration desk to sign in and pick up her key to their room. They were easily the most conspicuous people in the lobby—which Brenda rather enjoyed. The middle-aged woman clerk was decidedly cool, and unenthusiastic that Brenda was carrying only a briefcase rather than a suitcase. Andy finessed the clerk, calling her "honey" and "dear." They did not require a bellboy's assistance.

When they entered their 10th floor room, Andy started giggling, which quickly magnified into laughing.

"When I checked in this afternoon, they gave me a room that had twin beds. I went down and demanded a double bed."

"You didn't!" exclaimed Brenda, making wicked eyes. Better act sophisticated, she told herself.

"Yes, I told them we just had to have it—just so we could sleep in the same bed and maybe cuddle a little, of course."

"Oh, of course."

"You should have seen the reaction! But I got this anyway."

The room had *two* large double beds.

"I can't believe you had the guts to ask."

"Oh, I have plenty of guts."

They both laughed, almost hysterically.

"You can sleep in the other one if you want," Andy said.

"No, no, why should I?"

The room had a view of downtown Cleveland. After all, it was rather impressive at night—most cities are. Black buildings with a few twinkling lights are bound to look attractive.

They went scrounging off to look for a Coke machine and find the proper change. The Coke machine on their floor was broken, so they went down one floor and collected a number of Cokes. Andy showed Brenda how to put the Cokes on the air conditioner to keep them cool.

They sat on the small beige sofa near the window.

"How are you feeling physically?" Brenda had tried to hold off asking for as long as she could.

"Fine. Just couldn't be better."

"How's your head?"

"It's all right. I'm taking the anti-coagulants. I'm not supposed to drink much or get too excited. I don't mind about the drinking, but how am I supposed to not get excited? When I think about what happened, I get so angry."

"Of course you do. You've been through so much. I think it's amazing that you're still together, sitting here."

"I don't know how together I am. I keep forgetting things I used to know—I've forgotten some of the laws I used to use all the time in my job. My mind isn't there. I'm afraid I'll never be together again."

Andy began to cry. Brenda put her arms around her.

"Yes, you will."

They sat that way for hours. Andy cried. Brenda also cried some, stroked Andy's hair and her hot forehead, hugged her.

"I don't know what to do," Brenda finally said. "I don't know what you want me to do. Shall we just go to bed and sleep?"

Andy nodded.

They undressed to their underwear and lay down in one of the beds. For a long time they stayed quiet, with one's head on the other's shoulder, then they moved apart to sleep.

In the morning they rose fairly quickly and dressed for breakfast. Andy reached for a cigarette and Brenda fussed at her, "You mustn't do that with your blood clot. I'm sure it's not good for you."

"I'll be okay."

"Oh, of course, you're always okay."

"Sure, I am."

They went down to the coffee shop and ordered hamburgers and Cokes for breakfast.

"Order more. You're not eating enough."

"Yes, I am. I'm perfectly healthy. You're the one who isn't eating enough to keep up your strength."

"Looking at you ought to give me all the strength I need."

All writers mention eyes. You can't have a decent love affair in a novel without sparkling blue, melting brown, or intoxicating green eyes. Mentioning eyes is a cliché. But Andy's large brown eyes did not seem like clichés—their warm glance struck Brenda as the most beautiful thing she had ever seen. She felt as if she were going to fall off her chair (and they were sitting in a booth). Did Andy really mean to look at her *that* warmly?

"You're going to turn my head with that flattery. I'm just a simple, straightforward revolutionary lesbian and I don't know how to flirt. Women who flirt embarrass me."

"Huh," sniffed Andy. "You don't know how to flirt. With those bedroom eyes of yours—seems to me you're doing a pretty good job of flirting for someone who doesn't know how. I'll bet you flirt with those other writers on the paper all the time."

"Good grief, no, I'm considered a bit of a prude. Did you really say 'bedroom eyes'? My mother used to use that term—I never heard anyone else say it."

"Goodness gracious," she said in a little voice, "do I remind you of your mother?"

"In a way, you do. She's dark, too—darker than I am, anyway."

"Mine was light—almost as pale as you are. Had red hair."

They giggled.

"Maybe I won't be unattractive to you, then."

" 'Maybe I won't be unattractive to you' she says—I'm nearly falling out of my seat and she says maybe she isn't unattractive. Oh, you're a flirt all right. Probably lots of women have fallen in love with you."

Brenda winced. "No, they haven't. I wish they had. It's always the other way around—so much so that I'm embarrassed to talk about it. Let's talk about something else less heavy—like the revolution."

They laughed. "Right on, the revolution," Andy said.

"My terrible secret is that I have a great deal of trouble believing that there is going to be a literal revolution—a real overthrow of the government—in this country. I can imagine that happening only if there was another great depression, or similar chaos, and, given this country's history, I think fascists would be more likely to succeed than the left. Do you think I'm horrible for thinking that?" I don't want to get involved with someone who's going to put me down for not being socialist enough—might as well feel out her politics, Brenda thought.

"Horrible? Is it horrible to have sense? I think you're right. I don't trust people who talk big—who yell at you if you don't scream 'power to the people' as loud as they do."

"Pardon me, what am I doing? Making speeches at you after all you've been through. I'm sorry." What the hell do you think you're doing, she said to herself. Stop trying so hard to be impressive—but I'm not sure that I always knew the difference between trying to be sincere and trying to be impressive—and don't tell me anyone can be sincere—or anything else—without trying, without effort—I don't believe it.

"Don't be sorry. I want to hear what you think. You've thought about all these things a lot, I guess."

When they finished eating, Brenda asked where she could buy a newspaper. "I hate to admit it, but I'm totally addicted to newspapers—I want to know as much as I can about what's happening. Some radical—I'm fascinated by straight American politics—I want to know what every Congressional committee is doing."

"I like newspapers, too. We can get some papers at the drugstore and bring them back to the room to read."

They walked out into the city—it was much uglier by day than by night. Gray concrete was everywhere—little green. How depressing it must be for Andy to live there, Brenda thought. Tacky signs were the only relief from the gray.

She enjoyed walking beside Andy, being guided by Andy, watching Andy walk through her city. The strength of this small woman, absolutely undaunted by the tall, grim city, was amazing. In one of the gray buildings, she worked. In another, she had been raped and tortured. Here she was, walking brightly past the concrete monoliths that bore witness to a dull civilization; she bore witness to something else.

"I usually don't go through red lights, period. No more of this suicide stuff," Brenda chided.

"Nothing could be further from my mind."

They bought several papers.

They returned to the room and read awhile. They had risen late, and lunched long—it was already pretty late in the afternoon. Andy sat on the beige sofa, while Brenda sat in a large chair. After she finished a paper—in one of her less thorough readings—she could not take her thoughts off Andy.

"Mind if I sit there with you?" Brenda ventured.

"Why would you ever want to do that?" But she moved over.

Brenda sat down and put an arm around Andy and kissed her, very lightly, on the mouth.

Soft kisses, hugs, and strokes were exchanged.

Please let me do the right thing, Brenda thought. Am I doing the right thing by getting involved with her? I can't ever let her down, after all she has been through.

Tears welled onto Andy's cheeks.

"Are you all right?"

"I'm all right."

"Andy. Dear, dear Andy." She stroked her breasts. "Do you want to lie down?"

"No."

So they sat there, fully dressed in their pants and turtlenecks. Brenda slipped her hand between Andy's legs and rubbed softly on the crotch.

"Oh, Brenda." Sighing.

She kissed her, held her, rubbed her. Careful, ever so careful, worried about hurting her. Slipped her hand beneath the pants and rubbed.

"Oh Brenda, oh Brenda." Andy relaxed under her hand. They were both in tears. Brenda folded her in her arms and they sat, clinging to one another.

"Dear, sweet Andy. I hope I did the right thing."

"Oh, you did. I can't believe it. I haven't felt anything like this in so long. I didn't think I could feel this way again."

"I'm glad. I'm so glad."

In a while Brenda said, "Why don't we lie down and be more comfortable?"

"Oh, sure. After that." They smiled and started lying down.

"I want to make love to you this way."

"No, you can't, I haven't made love to you yet."

"That's all right. That doesn't matter." She was trying to slip Andy's clothes off.

"I shouldn't let you do the lovemaking again."

"Oh, don't be silly. I want to."

Andy put her head back, almost bumping the headboard. Brenda's hands rushed behind her head to cushion it. "Be careful."

Andy was more beautiful than anyone she had ever seen. Such a perfect color—brown was so much prettier than pink. Dark nipples. Short, sweet brown legs—so cuddly, her whole self was so cuddly. Curly dark hair—dark and small like the ideal best friend, Diana in the *Anne of Green Gables* books of her childhood. Small and dark like her black-haired favorite doll, Goo. So beautiful—she was being allowed to touch such a dear, beautiful woman.

Long, deep recent scars gashed across the thighs, some of them terminating near the vagina, some near the anus. They had violated this sweet, lovely woman—cut across the beauty. Forced ugliness on her. Brenda felt a momentary rush of anger, but suppressed it, thinking, no, she needs my affection, not my anger.

"Does it hurt if I touch you? Please let me know if I hurt."

"It's all right. You aren't hurting me."

"What about the clot? Should we be doing this?"

"It's okay. I asked the doctor if I could." She grinned.

"You asked her? Wicked lady! Oh, you're so beautiful! Do you know how beautiful you are?"

"Me? No."

"You're the most beautiful woman I've ever seen. Oh, your sweet curly hair. I want to kiss everything."

She kissed her neck, her eyebrows, eyelids, forehead, cheeks —every inch of her face. They kissed with soft, clinging, dizzy-making kisses. Brenda kissed shoulders, arms, elbows, hands, fingers, meeting every part. Andy was soft, fragrant. She even kissed her feet.

"Hey. What are you doing, silly?"

"Kissing your feet, silly. I want to know all of you." She stroked the legs, then went back and stroked the breasts. She sucked them.

"I never thought breasts were particularly beautiful before, Andy, but yours are."

"Oh, really."

They kissed.

She parted the hair, gently, and found small dark folds of skin that she sucked and kissed, learning every part. "You look like an oyster. I want to call this your oyster." Tasting, rejoicing—she had never felt so wonderful as when Andy moved under her.

When Andy came, she felt her own body dizzy with joy—no one else's body had she felt as her own—never had she felt so united.

"May I lie on top of you?"

"Oh, honey." Andy smiled briefly, closed her eyes, and lay there.

Brenda moved gently on top of her, feeling the radiating Andy who had just come from her tongue.

"Dear, precious Andy." She lay her cheek on Andy's cheek. It was impossible that there could be this much peace and joy in the world.

After they had lain there for a while, Andy said, "I want to make love to you now."

"Only if you want to. It's all right if you don't."

Happiness like this is so rare—how many days of my life have been this happy? Brenda remembered that this was the anniversary of the day she had first felt a mutual connection with Ted, five years before. Her mind paused, contemplating guilt, and passed over it. No, Andy was too fine to be clouded by her guilts to something that was over. She must bury her guilt over Ted, while acknowledging that she was an imperfect enough creature to have hurt another. Andy was the present and the future.

"Andy, I'm so happy."

Eventually, she said, "It's all right if I don't come, dear. I often don't. Everything feels wonderful and I'm so happy."

"I feel bad that I didn't make you come."

"No, no, don't feel that way. It doesn't matter."

They cuddled in one another's arms.

Before they went to sleep, Brenda said, "I must say goodnight to every part of your body," dived under the cover, and emerged by Andy's toes. "Goodnight, toes," she cried, kissing them.

"What on earth are you doing?" Andy fussed warmly.

"Why, it would be very rude of me not to say goodnight to every pretty part of my beautiful Andy's body. I don't want to offend any part."

"Kissing my feet! Oh, you're impossible!"

"Goodnight legs! Mmh." She stroked them—"and goodnight, clit . . ."

"Whoa, you keep out of there, silly. I'm going to sleep."

"I'll just help you sleep, dear. A few little strokes."

"Move on!"

"Oh, all right. Sorry, clit. Andy doesn't understand you. She said we must part for the night. Goodnight, breasts."

"Oh my goodness!"

"Pay no attention, I'm just saying goodnight to your breasts."

"Uh huh. Come up here, idiot, and kiss me."

They slept peacefully. In the morning, Brenda said, "This is the first night in a year that I've slept without a sleeping pill."

"Imagine that."

"Let's make love right away."

"Brenda, you're so bad."

"Those are my initials, you know. B.A.D. I've always liked them—partly because I've always been such a goodie-goodie. Are you afraid of a wicked woman like me with initials like that?"

"Petrified! You 'Bad'—that's the cutest thing, oh Bad, I love you. You sweet punkin."

"Punkin—as in 'pumpkin'—my mother used to call me that. Oh, how is it that you know all these phrases that only my mother uses."

Brenda was thrilled enough to burst. She had wanted all her life to be called "Bad," but nobody ever did call her that. Andy seemed to have some connection with her oldest memories—how else could she come up with phrases like "bedroom eyes" and "punkin." It must mean that Andy was the special one for her—they were destined for each other.

"I love you, Bad."

"I care so much about you, Andy," she said—but she felt much more.

She loves me! I don't want to be cold, but I must be absolutely honest. I must, must be absolutely committed to her. No backing out now. She must be able to count on me. She loves me—she's so vulnerable, has been hurt so much—I must not have any defenses against her. There must be no barriers.

They giggled and cuddled. Andy pretended to hide from her under the sheets, and Brenda went burrowing after to find her.

Andy decreed that they must go to have a meal at the hotel restaurant.

"But I'm not hungry. I'm only hungry for you."

"I know, I know. That's why we have to have some rest."

They went down to the restaurant, not taking their eyes off one another for a second. They could barely eat. Bad tried to see how many passionate or sexual things she could say while the waitress was just out of earshot.

"This food tastes so bland compared to your oyster. I love your oyster."

"My goodness gracious, you really are bad. And I thought you were such a lady."

Each would look at the other intensely, just as she was about to eat a bite or to swallow, preventing her from wanting to.

Andy tried to light a cigarette and Bad kept staring at her until she hid behind a menu to light it.

"Take care of yourself, honey."

"I will, Bad, I will."

When they walked out to buy the newspapers, Brenda felt spectacular. If she had felt comfortable walking with Andy before, she beamed with pride now. She wanted to scream, World! This woman loves me! See how lucky I am.

Andy giggled. "You keep walking on my left side, to protect me."

"Do I?"

"You certainly do. Every time we come to another street you maneuver so that you'll be on the street side."

"I'm sorry if it bothers you. I didn't notice."

"That's all right. It's cute. But Bad, honey, I can probably fight better than you can if we ever had to. I'm small, but I make a pretty good fist."

"I'll bet you do."

But she kept on walking on the left side. Forgive me if I'm being male, she thought, but it's true. I do want to protect her.

It was getting to be time to call Ted and tell him that she was all right—he would be worried.

"Please don't mind," she told Andy. "I haven't touched him in a year and a half—I would never sleep with him again. He knows I'm a lesbian. I'm still fond of him and I'd like to be friends always. He's been supportive when women have hurt me, even though he's obviously hurting too."

"Oh, you belong to Ted."

"Oh, God, Andy, don't say such a thing. I don't belong to Ted—I belong to you. There's no question about that. But I do feel guilty towards him, he has been kind—and put me through grad school. If I could love a man with my deepest love, if I could make a permanent commitment to a man, I would make one to him—but I can't and won't—and I feel shitty about revising my commitments. I'm worried because he has become such a homebody that he just sits and broods while I go out to meetings—or come here. He's got to find a life of his own. I do want to be as decent as possible under the circumstances, although I wouldn't say my behavior towards him is decent in general. I wouldn't want to be involved with someone who would totally hate him—I don't think you would, would you?"

"Oh, no, sounds like he's okay. I'll be nice to Ted. You are married to him, so I guess he's more important. You aren't hiding him—I just want to know where I stand."

Brenda choked and started feeling hysterical. "No, no, damnit. I'm going to get a divorce, Andy. I've been talking about it for a year. I just would like to wait a few more months 'til I take my last Ph.D. exams, and then I'll get a job with a decent salary and support myself at last. The exam's in November—I'd like to separate from him in January. Is that too long? Is that too calculated? Do you want me to leave him immediately? Do you want me to stay in Cleveland?"

"No, Bad, that would be ree-diculous. I don't want you to move here—I'll move to Washington as soon as my health gets cleared up."

"Oh, honey, I'm so scared about the blood clot. If you want me to stay here with you every minute, I will."

"Don't be silly. I have to work. I'm living at my grandmother's. I know you don't want to leave the newspaper."

That was true, damnit. She loathed the sight of this ugly city—she was terrified at the thought of messing up the Ph.D. at this stage—and the newspaper—she couldn't bear to stay away from it even for a week.

"There are doctors in Washington, too. Can't you move there now?"

"Not yet, honey."

Brenda called Ted while Andy was sitting next to her, in the hotel room. "Hello, Ted. Sorry I didn't call sooner. I'm doing fine."

"Good. I thought you would. How's Andy?" His voice was boisterous, phony hearty.

"She's a wonderful person." This was surrealistic.

"Good. How's Cleveland?"

"Hideous. How's the cat?"

"He's doing fine. He misses you so much that he keeps coming over to me and purring."

"Poor little thing." (She meant the cat.)

"He and I are getting along fine." His voice started getting lugubrious. "We've been sitting in the living room and I've been reading *David Copperfield*. I was crying about Little Emily a while ago." For the past six months, he had been reading Dickens—was determined to read every book Dickens ever wrote. Dickens was the only non-science fiction novelist he would read.

Out of perversity, Brenda had decided that Dickens was the only novelist she wouldn't read. She was already sentimental about "A Christmas Carol"—that was bad enough. And she liked Fagin and Nancy in *Oliver Twist*. There must have been something good in Dickens, since Dostoievsky liked him. "More Dickens," she said, not enthusiastically.

"I know you don't appreciate him. This morning I walked over to Hechingers and bought a new drill bit so I could hang the bicycle rack. Then I worked on that a few hours. And I'm making chili for dinner—with stew meat in it. I'm putting in a whole can of jalapenos since you aren't here."

"Ugh, sounds a little hot."

"I think it's the best chili I've ever made. You're really missing something. I'll save some for you. When are you coming home?"

"Well, I guess I'll go back to Washington tomorrow; there's a lot of work to be done at the office. It's time for our bulk billing to bookstores."

"Good. I'll see you then."

"Okay. Good-bye. Have a nice dinner."

She hung up. "That felt so weird. Like another world. I will tell him about you."

Andy was smiling. Did she really mean the smile? Did she understand how secure she was?

"It's okay. You don't have to."

"I want to. Andy, I will stay if you want. Please understand that I'm serious about you. After all you've been through, I never would have made love if I wasn't serious."

"I know you're serious, honey."

"Sure you don't want me to stay?"

"*Bad*, I *have* to go to *work* tomorrow." Andy spoke in a caressing tone, with an affectionate stress on almost every word.

"I hope all this sex hasn't hurt your dear little head."

"No, silly. My little head feels just fine—and so does the rest of me."

They kissed, but they went to dinner to punctuate the call to Ted, separate it from their lovemaking.

Andy tried to pay for dinner.

"No, you don't. You paid for lunch. I'll pay for dinner."

"No, you won't. Dinner is more expensive."

"That's all right, let me get it."

"No, you don't, Bad."

"Then we'll pay separately."

"Oh, you're im*pos*sible."

The next morning, she found that Andy had already paid for the room. "Andy! You'll have to take my half of the money."

"No, no. It's my city, my treat."

"A little treating is okay, but that's too much."

They squabbled a bit, but they probably wound up paying similar amounts. Brenda preferred their attitude to that of people who have to tally up every cent, and worry about paying an extra dime. They were both obsessed with giving presents, as it turned out.

The last morning was hard—they were both too upset about parting to make love.

"I will stay if . . . "

"No, you don't, honey. Get out of bed and get dressed."

She kissed Andy's hand, her shoulder, any part of her that could be found while they got dressed.

They sank into one of their soft kisses that made them both dizzy.

"You are being wicked, Bad. Get ready or you'll miss your bus."

"I don't care if I miss my bus." She knew that for all of Andy's fussing to get her to leave, she would feel deserted when Brenda actually left.

"I want to come back this weekend. Is that all right?"

"I don't know. Maybe."

"Can't we make it definite?"

Finally Andy blurted out, "I'm afraid I'll never see you again."

"Andy! You're going to see so much of me that I just won't let anybody else walk in front of your eyes, that's all."

"I hope so."

"I know so."

Andy went with her to the station and watched her get on the bus. They were both a little teary.

"Please trust me. I'm really serious about you."

"Sure, honey. You like me. Maybe you'll find someone you like better, another writer."

"No, I won't. I'll see you soon."

I must learn how to reassure her, Brenda thought on the bus trip back to Washington. Again, she could not read because her thoughts were so full of Andy. It suddenly hit her: Andy is the *one*. The woman I've been waiting for. I don't care who disapproves of seeing love in those terms—I do see it that way. I might be able to kiss her every day, wake up beside her every morning—even going grocery shopping with her would be joyous, joking—with Ted, it's depressing. I love her. I should have told her I love her.

Of course it takes a certain egoism to believe that most of yourself will be loved and respected, and the rest forgiven; it did not occur to her that Andy might not have that kind of egoism: if Andy felt she had to keep up certain barriers, that was a species of illness, if not outright cruelty.

The first thing Brenda did when she arrived in Washington was to go to a florist and send yellow roses to Andy, signing them "Doug" so her grandmother wouldn't know they were from a woman. Having no interest in anything but Andy, Brenda wrote a letter.

Dearest Andy Love,

Riding home on the bus, I realized that you are the One (and Only). You are *it*. I am so grateful that I have found you.

I think we must have been destined to meet. You are my destiny — wonderful, perfect destiny. I am so lucky.

I love you. Thank you for telling me you loved me. Pardon me for not telling you sooner that I love you. But please believe that I do.

You are so sweet—your every gesture is adorable. You are the most beautiful woman I have ever seen. I have never felt so full of joy and laughter as when I am with you. You are so funny—so tender.

I want to be with you always, dearest. I hope that we can be together. Being away from you these hours feels so strange—but the hours are filled with you anyway.

Love,
Your Bad

It was hard sitting down to eat chili with Ted that night—being with him seemed considerably more awful than it used to. She still carried the sense of Andy's body, and his presence was an intrusion. She couldn't bring herself to tell him about Andy, because his knowledge would be an intrusion, too. All she said was that Andy was a good, friendly, witty woman. She didn't want to face his reaction—she wanted to hold Andy privately. God, why had she stayed in this apartment so long, why did she have to see a man walk around half naked in his bathrobe? For the first time, a tinge of physical revulsion awakened.

8

As soon as she arrived at work in the morning, Brenda called Andy at her office. "How are you?"

"Oh, fine."

"I miss you."

"*You* miss *me*? Do you have any idea how lonesome this town is since you left? I'm glad to see you remember me."

"*Remember* you? What the hell are you saying? I haven't thought of anything but you."

"I hope I see you again, Bad."

"Of course you will! You can't keep me away!"

"Oh, I can't but maybe someone else could."

"What do you mean?"

"I just get upset easily now. I saw this man in the street today . . . "

"Yes, go on."

"I probably shouldn't, but I guess I have to now. Well, he was somebody I had seen in the mental ward. He recognized me. I thought maybe he was following me."

"No, darling, no!"

"Maybe I'm getting paranoid, but those dudes scare me. I don't know if there's any way they could get me back there. I'd rather die."

"No, they mustn't get you again. They won't. I love you, Andy, I should have told you that this weekend."

"You don't have to say that, honey."

"But it's true, I tell you, it's true. I've never felt this way about anyone in my life—thrilled and committed at the same time. I love you."

"It's sweet of you to say that." The voice was softer.

"It's not sweet, it's true. I love you, Andy."

"I love you, Bad."

"Do talk to a lawyer or somebody if you think there's a chance the people from the hospital could cause you trouble."

"Maybe I will."

Brenda worried all day and a good part of the night. She told Ted that her friend Andy might be facing some trouble with people from the hospital and that she would probably go back to Cleveland that weekend. He readily agreed—causing her to feel more guilt, though guilt toward Ted seemed a petty emotion compared with Andy's problems and their love.

The minute that Dolly walked into the office, Brenda said, "Well, I met Andy and fell in love with her."

Dolly's face and voice were controlled, showing her almost professional cheerfulness. "I'm not surprised."

"She's wonderful—much more than I could ever have imagined. She's so warm. Everything she does is adorable. Oh, Dolly, she loves me, too."

"That isn't surprising. You've been good to her."

"No, no, everything is completely different between us. I don't want her to love me because I've 'been good' to her. We have so much in common—we joke the same, we're both silly, romantic and unashamed to be that way—I can't imagine being able to be as silly with the women on the paper as I can be with her. I love the part of myself that I can be with her."

"That's good. I hope you'll have a nice relationship. Don't get too serious too soon, though." Dolly always advocated "keeping things casual."

"Me? Don't be ridiculous! I'm serious already. I want to be with her forever."

Dolly groaned. "Yech. I don't believe in love."

"There are times, much as I adore you, when I'm glad you're not a lesbian. Perhaps that's why you're not. Maybe you have to believe in love to go to the trouble of becoming a lesbian."

"I'll never come out then."

"You don't know what you're missing. The days I've been with Andy have been the best days of my life. I can't think of anything but her." She proceeded to give Dolly a recitation about Andy's endearing qualities and expressions. Dolly was politely enthusiastic.

Later in the day, while Brenda was talking on the phone with Andy, Nina came by the office to do some typing.

Brenda was a little agitated because Andy had just talked to a radical lawyer, but was still apprehensive and convinced that she was being followed. The lawyer had told her that their guild would keep in close touch with her.

Brenda walked over to Nina. "Have you heard that I'm involved with Andy?"

"Dolly just told me while you were on the phone." Nina looked tense.

"She's so sweet and affectionate. I can't wait for her to meet you."

"Is she coming to Washington?"

"Soon, I hope. She says she plans to move here."

"Good."

"I'm worried about her, though. She's worried now that some man from the mental ward might be following her. And I'm worried about the blood clot . . . "

Nina became so agitated that she looked as if she was going to burst. "Don't tell me about it. I just don't believe anything she says. Too much has happened to her. It just isn't real. Please don't get me wrong, Brenda. I do believe you. I'm sure you're telling me what she says. I just don't believe her. I think you ought to be careful."

The impact of this blow was physical. Brenda staggered.

"You can't talk that way about the woman I love."

"I'm sorry, that's what I think. I don't want to talk about her."

"I saw her scars, for God's sake."

"I'm not saying that nothing happened to her. I'm sure something did. She's very disturbed."

"How can you have so little compassion? You, of all people, who have been suicidal yourself? And put in a mental ward? You remember the social workers said they might have used shocks on you if we hadn't found a decent doctor? How can you dismiss another woman's suffering that way?" Her voice was shaking with pain and anger.

Nina's face became a deeper scarlet. "It's what I think."

"It is all pretty far out," Dolly chimed in. "Crazy people can be really delightful, charming. I've seen lots of them."

"She isn't crazy. Fine radical feminists you are. You only believe Joann Little because you've read about her in the *New York Times*. Andy isn't in the *New York Times*, so you don't believe her. I love her."

Shaking violently, she walked out of the office. I may never come back, she thought. I hate them. My two best friends on the paper. This insult is too terrible. Racists. Classists. Can't recognize the voice of real suffering. How dare they try to turn me against her. Andy, you're so much better than all of them.

It had never occurred to her that she would walk away from the newspaper. She had stayed through political and personal misery, sure that she would remain, that this was where she should be working and that she would never leave unless the paper folded—a circumstance she would do anything she could to prevent. Only her closest friends could give her this much pain—no other woman's insult or attack would ever cause her to leave. If she had to choose between the paper and Andy, she would choose Andy.

She would take the next bus to Cleveland. First, she went home, to cash a check and call Andy.

"Please let me come there, Andy. Not to support you, but because I need you to support me. Something awful happened. I hate to tell you, maybe I should hide it from you, but I'm in so much pain that I can't. My friends Nina and Dolly don't believe what you say; they think you're making things up."

"I wish I were making things up." Her tone was slightly bitter.

"Please don't hate them, they are good people—I think I half hate them myself. How could they turn this skeptical eye on your suffering? They're carrying being reporters too far. I don't know whether I can work with them anymore—maybe I'll leave the paper."

"Bad! You mustn't do that, honey. You'd be miserable without the paper. It's so important to you." Andy was soothing.

"Not as important as you are. Andy, I know it's only Thursday, but please let me come to Cleveland tonight. I need you."

"All right."

Thursday was the newspaper's meeting night. Brenda called Ted and asked him not to answer the phone—she wanted Nina and Dolly to worry about her. Brenda was so obsessed about meetings that her unexplained absence from a meeting was the strongest thing she could do short of resigning. Let Nina worry. Dolly wasn't a worrier, but Nina was.

When challenged, Brenda felt sure that Andy was essentially good and lovable, that some connection between the two of them was deeper, more tender, closer to perfect communication than anything she had ever experienced. Even if nothing Andy said about her background or about particular episodes had been literally true, that essential inner person was so true that literal truthfulness did not matter. Indeed, Brenda thought, Andy probably was telling the truth, but that was irrelevant. Nothing that had happened in their lives up to that point mattered in comparison to the connection between Andy and Bad.

She arrived at the Cleveland station late and hunted worriedly. What if someone was following Andy and had captured her? There she was. Thank God. The two and a half days they had been apart seemed like weeks. They hugged, and went off to the hotel. It was raining hard; it often rains in Cleveland.

A driver in a passing cab yelled at their cab driver, "Those women yours?"

The driver made a negative gesture.

They were both disgusted that anyone had dared to think, even for a moment, that they could be part of a prostitution ring, but there wasn't any way that either could reply, could say, "Hey, this is my lover."

The room clerk at the hotel was less than delighted to see them again so soon. They had clearly become suspicious characters.

The moment they were in the room, Brenda was on her knees in front of Andy, hugging her.

"I'm so sorry for telling you about those people—or for telling them about you, since they don't understand. I've been so worried about you. I need to be with you."

"Bad, get up. Don't go down on your knees to me like that."

"Why not? It's a good position for hugging."

Andy stroked Brenda's hair. Her voice was husky. "I didn't believe you were ever coming back."

"Oh, honey, of course I'm back."

"My friends had problems about you, too. They've been telling me that I was crazy to get involved with a reporter. They said you'd just get my story, write about me, and never come back."

"What!" She sat back, astounded. "Me? What kind of reporter do they think I am? *Womanpaper* isn't exactly *Time* magazine. We don't run around the country seducing young women to get their stories. Didn't you tell them I mostly write book reviews?"

"They haven't read the paper, so they don't know quite what it's like. They're just worried about me. You're white, too."

"That! Oh, damn them."

"It's all right, Bad. They aren't all too crazy about white people."

"I hope they'll trust me when they get to know me."

"Getting them to know you may be the problem. My friend

Gerri—she's this very butch type who's been a friend since we were kids—was very angry. Very sure you were going to hurt me. Others are friends of Maxy's and they trusted her, but they're going to be kind of critical of anyone else."

"Oh, great. Well, we're even. Nobody's friends trust anybody. But I'm not as angry about your friends—though they scare me. I suppose it makes sense for them to distrust whites. I don't know if I can ever forgive my friends though."

"Yes, you will, honey. They're your friends."

"Didn't it hurt you?"

"It hurts, but I'm okay."

On Friday, Andy took off from work to stay in the hotel room.

Brenda felt something in herself holding back in lovemaking, something that she felt she had to confess.

"Andy?" she asked as they sat on the bed, pretending to read.

"Yes?"

"Something is bothering me."

"Yes?"

"The worst part about the things Nina and Dolly said was that they shook me, gave me a tiny seed of doubt that never existed before. I came here hoping to find thugs tailing you. I looked at your bottle of pills, and saw that it did say 'anti-coagulants.' I wanted to have some kind of 'proof' to take back to them. Forgive me, honey. I was stupid."

Andy's whole body shook. She threw herself on her stomach and hid her face with her arms, sobbing.

"Oh my God, I'm sorry. Oh God, I hurt you more. Forgive me, Andy, I love you." She tried to stroke Andy's shoulders and hair, but Andy's body was tense, unyielding.

"Please look at me, honey. Say something."

There was no response but sobs.

Brenda was terrified. Oh God, I've lost her. Please, please, don't let me lose her.

"Forgive me, please. I love you. Oh, please, say something."

"Not you, Bad, not you, too," she choked.

There was nothing to do but sit there, stroking sometimes, apologizing sometimes. When the tears stopped, Andy continued to lie there, unwilling to look at her.

"Please forgive me. I don't forgive myself. Doubting Thomas was forgiven."

After nearly an hour with no response, Brenda slunk to a chair and curled up in it. She wrote a note apologizing, and passed it to Andy.

Half an hour later, Andy forgave her.

Every cliché Brenda had heard about forgiveness or redemption—and growing up Catholic, she had heard many—passed through her mind. Stupid Thomas—she had already seen the wounds in the side, so there was no excuse for her.

Religious phrases crowded into her head. Perhaps, she thought, I should resist—but she didn't. Andy was her suffering hero who had gone beyond suffering to strength. A lesbian martyr who had escaped death, who, after tortures, had kept the faith.

That evening they talked about religion.

"As a child, I was obsessed by the church," said Brenda. "Nuns were women who rejected me, led lives that were more concerned with the important things in life—God, love, being a lady—than people who lived in houses and were concerned about buying cars and going to the supermarket. Nuns were the most impressive women I met—one of the lay teachers at our school used to say that if you threw a broomstick with a habit on it into a classroom the children would curtsey. I was slightly afraid because they were stern, but I worshipped this one elderly nun who would tell us stories of her youth. She believed that being a saint was the same as being a lady—with a few more prayers thrown in."

"I loved nuns, too. I went to a Catholic school for a while. Part of my family was Catholic and part of it was Baptist, so I was both. Baptist for a few years, Catholic for a few years."

"Did religion make you feel guilty?"

Andy curled up on the bed. "Did I feel guilty! I was the guiltiest. I'm still the guiltiest. When I was in the hospital those years when I was a teenager, I asked God to heal me and promised that if he did I would try to be a good person. Then, when I had feelings about the nurses—one of them would kiss me and touch me—I felt so guilty. I tried not to have sinful thoughts about women, but I had them."

Brenda was a little frightened by this revelation. "You thought loving women was sinful? I never thought that! Women were holy—being in love with my classmates was part of my sacred vocation to become a nun. It was spiritual love, I was sure. I combined praying to the Lord with glancing about the chapel at them, had the same feeling of exaltation about them and God and prayed for them. 'Lord, let Colleen be able to live a good and holy life, and be happy'—that sort of thing. I never let myself have more specifically sexual fantasies about them—never was conscious of wanting to. My more graphic sexual fantasies were about men—that was the sinful lust I felt guilty about. Women's weren't. See, I was a good lesbian feminist even then." She giggled.

Andy sighed. "You were lucky. Even now I feel guilty sometimes. Oh, I know you'll tell me I shouldn't feel that, but I do."

Brenda determined to chase the troubling feeling away by levity. "Andy, Andy. How can you blaspheme about the devotion to St. Lesbiana? Don't you know what a good, sweet saint she is? I am a *very* devout follower of hers."

"I'll bet you are."

"Why, certainly I am. St. Lesbiana is a fine saint. A Virgin, not Martyr. She spent her life—she lived as the Holy Roman Empire waned into the middle ages—illuminating the poems of Sappho for the sisters in her abbey. St. Lesbiana could perform many wonders—she spoke in tongues, she practiced the laying on of hands."

"Bad!" Andy pretended to be scandalized.

"Have you never heard of the laying on of hands, my dear?" she asked, lurching across the bed and stroking Andy's nearest leg.

Andy put on an itty-bitty voice. "Goodness gracious, such things from a saint." She made a gesture to indicate brushing away such worldly pursuits.

"Very holy, dearest Andy, very holy."

"I can see how holy it is."

"The kiss of peace, sweet sister." She gave Andy one of their favorite long, soft kisses.

"Peace! That isn't peaceful, Bad. It knocks me out."

"Repent, Sinner, and join the devotion of St. Lesbiana. St. Lesbiana is calling you." She stroked Andy's crotch.

"No, no, we have to eat dinner. I can't let you starve yourself."

"Andy, my faith is great. I am willing to fast, even unto starvation, in the service of St. Lesbiana."

"Uh huh. I'm impressed with your religiousness, Bad."

"Oh come, all ye faithful," she crooned, stroking. "Come to St. Lesbiana."

"Come! I've come three times today already!"

"The spirit can come an infinite number of times."

"No, it can't. Not to me."

"Your faith is shaky. But you have loved much."

"You've loved pretty much, too."

"But I shall love more. The spirit of love knows no limits."

"Oh, really? Well, Bad, mine knows limits." She jumped up and sat in a chair. They both laughed almost hard enough to fall on the floor.

"I kneel before you, holy acolyte of St. Lesbiana." Brenda flopped on her knees beside the chair and threw her arms around Andy.

"Were you really that religious when you were growing up?" Brenda asked her later.

"Religious? Why, I was so religious that I smashed my grandmother's entire record collection when I heard that profane music and dance were creations of the devil."

"You didn't!" She was a little more horrified than she wanted to admit.

"I did."

"That must have been when you were a Baptist."

"Uh huh."

"Catholics don't go for excesses like that. The farthest I ever went was to make a little whip to flagellate myself when I sinned, but I stopped when I found out it hurt."

Andy chuckled. "I've done that, too. Probably still ought to."

"Andy! Don't you dare hurt your precious body. I won't stand for it! Do you hear that, body?" she cried, grabbing Andy's foot. "Do you hear what silly old Andy wants to do to you? Don't worry, body, I won't let her—I'm on your body's side." She rubbed Andy's side.

"You sure are, honey."

"Precious—that suits you—I'll call you 'presh' for short."

She had made love to Andy twice in a row and was trying to a third time. "No, you don't, it's my turn to make love to you, pumpkin."

Brenda settled in to feeling wonderful whenever she was called "pumpkin." She shivered with pride that Andy really wanted to touch her.

They embraced and embraced, and then she lay there, her body shaking, her head buzzing, her feet numb. "God, I think my head's going to burst."

"That's all right." Andy giggled and continued licking.

Brenda trembled. "I don't believe it. Well, I'll die happy," her voice stammered.

Waves of intense feeling poured through her.

"Andy," she cried. There were no other images, no fantasies.

There was nothing but Andy.

Andy had a drink at dinner—which her doctor had forbidden —and soon lay on the bed, sick and sweating.

Brenda sat on the side of the bed, her whole body tense with anticipation. The minutes were hours. Her eyes devoured Andy.

"Are you all right? Can't I call the doctor?"

"No, it's all right, Bad."

"It isn't. Your forehead's covered with sweat. Can I bring you a cool cloth." She did this. "Are you sure I can't call the doctor, just in case?"

"No, don't worry, honey."

Long silences interrupted these brief spurts of conversation.

"Is there a pain in your head?"

"Some."

"Oh God."

"It's okay."

Oh let her not be dying before my eyes, please. But better that we be together.

They held hands at times.

Andy's eyes were closed most of the time. When they were open, a confused, desperate trace of pain was unmistakable, although her voice tried to deny it.

After an hour or so, she stopped sweating. In another half hour, she was sure that she was better, that nothing was the matter. Andy started speaking in her fast, cheerful tone, insisting that everything was cool and had never been cooler.

Brenda had seen a hundred funerals and felt the guilt for not getting a doctor, not helping enough. "I've been so frightened."

"Me, too, honey." Andy slowed down her voice. "What a terrible time to go. I couldn't stand the thought of leaving you here in a hotel room. Ugh! It's awful. I guess it was just the medicine and the alcohol."

"Please don't drink again, baby. Please take care of your sweet head," said Brenda, kissing her forehead. How was it possible to be so happy in the midst of this fear? Wasn't she selfish to keep thinking about making love, to keep forgetting about Andy's health?

Andy was feeling better on Sunday, and they made love again, although Brenda was a little more frightened about the possible consequences. She had visions of bursting a blood vessel. All was well, though, and quiet. They read the papers, worried together about Joann Little's trial for murder of her jailer.

Brenda was more reluctant than ever to leave. "I don't know whether I want to go back. I don't know whether I want to go back to the newspaper. I don't want to see Dolly and Nina. I don't want to leave you when you're sick. My place is with you."

"No, no, Bad. You love the newspaper."

"I can take a leave of absence."

"No, don't be silly, of course not. I won't let you."

"Well, you realize this time that I'm coming back, don't you? That I'll be back next weekend?"

"Of course. You'll never be able to get away from my fabulous lovemaking."

They planned a future together.

"We'll be lifetime lovers," said Andy.

"Of course."

They would live together and leave love notes for each other all over the house, hidden like Easter eggs. Getting tired of each other was impossible. They would become a wise old lesbian couple who kindly, platonically fostered young lesbians. Nothing in their lives could ever be routine because they would always be able to glance at each other and sink into one another's eyes.

"You will come and live in D.C., as soon as your head's cleared up, won't you, baby?"

Sometimes Andy would say, "Noth-ing could keep me away." Sometimes she'd say, "You sure you want me there?"

Brenda would have to clear Andy's name, get some respect for her. Andy was her lover. She would do anything to protect her, she felt. Even lie. If her friends didn't believe the truth, they didn't deserve the truth. Would it bother her—no. They had hurt her woman. The truth of Andy's basic goodness was more important than any mere detail.

She wrote Dolly and Nina notes—lying on paper would be easier, after all—and she wouldn't have to face any negative reactions—if she saw many more of their negative reactions, her feelings for them would recede further and further. A letter was cowardly, but probably most effective.

Each note said:

I love Andy. She is a wonderful person. She and I are going to be together for a long time, so it's important that my friends respect her.

You have been mistaken about her. I have gone with her to her doctor and her lawyer, and everything is as she says. Please stop saying disparaging things about her.

We have had a good friendship and I would hate to lose it, but I shall never listen to attacks on the woman I love.

Nina called her up and apologized. "I'm glad you're right, Brenda. I didn't want to be right. I just had to say what I thought."

Dolly was more restrained—probably because she was more skeptical. She merely said, "I'm glad you like her. But don't get too carried away. I don't believe in romance."

Their responses were good enough to permit Brenda to work with them again. She eagerly communicated their responses to Andy, somewhat exaggerating their warmth and enthusiasm.

9

In their Thursday evening phone call, Andy said, "Listen, Bad, there's another problem. It's us, Bad."

" 'Us'? What's the matter with us? We're a great couple, a wonderful couple."

"That's what you say."

"Don't you think so?"

"You didn't believe me. You doubted me. I can't forget that."

Brenda felt as if she were falling off a cliff. "But you forgave me. I thought that was all settled."

"I thought so, too, but it isn't. Since you left, I've been thinking about it. Maybe you don't trust me. Maybe we aren't right for each other."

"Andy! You're the most important person in the world to me. Of course I trust you. Of course I love you. We're so happy together— how could anyone be happier than we are when we're together?"

"We *seem* happy, but what does it mean if you don't trust me?"

"I do trust you, Andy."

"I guess I don't believe that. You hurt me a lot. The more I think about it, the more it hurts."

"Let me come to Cleveland early this weekend, as soon as possible, and I'll make it up."

"I don't want you to come this weekend."

"Oh, no, don't cut me off, please. If we are having problems, we should be working on them together."

"I don't want to. My grandmother's going away and I just want to be alone."

"Honey, please."

"I don't think it would do any good."

Brenda was in a panic. Had she made some irretrievable mistake, committed some irreversible crime? How could anything be irreversible if you loved each other? She kept calling Andy but all of the calls were the same.

Early Friday morning, she hurried off on a Greyhound to Cleveland. Since Andy kept refusing her permission to come, she went without telling Andy. Perhaps making herself more completely vulnerable would move Andy. Brenda left Ted a note, scratched quickly on a piece of looseleaf paper, which said:

> Dear Ted,
>   I know that I haven't been able to treat you well, and I'm sorry. I apologize for hurting you, but I love Andy and I must go to her. She and I are lovers, though we are having problems. I know that nothing I can say will make things any easier for you. Hate me if you want, but I must do what I think is right.
>
>   Brenda

This bus ride was considerably less pleasant than the previous ones. There was no Andy to meet her at the station; she would have to call Andy and hope for luck. Surely Andy couldn't refuse to meet her after she was already there.

She read a Heinrich Boll novel about living under the Nazis. A child was being "sacrificed," and Catholic Boll was constantly making "Lamb of God" references.

Remember that Andy, too, has been a "Lamb of God," she told herself. Never forget how much she has suffered. She has a right to be indignant when her suffering is not respected.

Brenda was excited by the time she reached the station. She will see me, she will. She will forgive me.

It was about five o'clock. Andy usually stayed at work later than that. Brenda rushed to a pay phone, and dialed. No—Andy had left work, she was attending a meeting.

Brenda sat in the station, reading her book. Until you end victimization, the only possible way of life is siding with the victims.

She called Andy's home at six—just in case—but there was no answer.

At seven, she called again.

At eight, her tension was becoming more apparent.

She couldn't refrain from calling at eight-thirty.

She called at nine—the bums hanging around the station were

noticing how often she called. She felt alone, unloved, vulnerable.

At ten, the station guards noticed and watched her more closely.

At ten-thirty, Andy answered the phone. "I've been at a seminar on family law and I just got home. What's happening?"

"I'm in Cleveland."

"You're where? Oh, no, Bad."

"I'm in Cleveland, at the dear old Greyhound station. I didn't want the weekend to pass without seeing you."

"Oh no, why did you do such a crazy thing? There aren't any more buses going back to town tonight. I couldn't come even if I wanted to."

Brenda shuddered at the thought of spending the night in the station, then made up her mind to it.

"Oh well, I'm closer to you anyway. And we can talk on the phone without paying long distance rates."

"Oh, Bad, go back home."

"Why should I do a silly thing like that? I've come here, so I think I'll wait around until tomorrow. Maybe I can see you then."

"No, Bad. That's awful. I don't want you there all night! Why don't you take a bus back?"

"I'm afraid of the bus at night, even more than I am of the station, silly, so why should I do that?"

"You can't stay in the bus station all night!"

"Certainly I can. Lots of travelers do it. I'll admit it's a little creepy. I love you—I'd do worse things to be near you. I want to work things out."

"I don't think things can be worked out."

"Of course they can if we try."

"I just don't want to love somebody who doesn't trust me."

"Would I come all the way here and spend my night in the bus station for somebody I didn't trust? Maybe it's good if I spend the night in the station—I'll do penance for my sin against you."

"I don't want you to do penance."

"Well, it's all right. I could go to the Holiday Inn, anyway—I just don't want to spend all that money on a room unless we're going to be together. I can't afford thirty-six dollars for a little rest. I'll stay here."

"Oh, Bad! I feel awful about this."

"Good! I hope you'll feel awful enough to forgive me."

"It's not just forgiving you, it's whether we're right for each other."

"Of course we're right for each other. Who else is as silly as we are?"

She stood there talking until after midnight, then asked Andy if she didn't want to sleep.

"Sleep! While you're standing around a bus station? No, I shouldn't sleep."

"Well, I need to go to the bathroom and get another Coke to keep me awake. May I call you back later?"

"Sure—call me back later—to say good-bye. You really should leave on the two o'clock bus."

"I would like to go along with your wishes, dearest, but not in this."

There were fewer people in the station now, and more of them could be considered "creepy looking." She felt frightened, embarrassed, not as tough and self-confident as a lesbian feminist ought to feel. She wanted to be as inconspicuous as possible. The plastic seats were getting harder. She finished the Boll book and began one of Eli Wiesel's. She had read many of his before. A concentration camp survivor, he tried to find a capacity for continuing life and caring. He had lost his town—a whole town of people killed. But at least there were some other Jewish survivors—Andy didn't have any real peers. Wiesel kept saying how hard it was to be with people who had no understanding of what he had been through. Of course Andy must feel something similar, except that she could not even tell most people what she had gone through. And then to be doubted, challenged! And she, Brenda, was afraid of sitting all night in a bus station.

At ten minutes past two, she called Andy. "Hello. I hope I didn't wake you?"

"No, I'm awake. Don't tell me you didn't take the two o'clock bus?"

"No. I told you I'm afraid of the bus at night."

"Well, you can take the six-thirty bus then."

"If you still won't see me."

"No, I won't. I'm not up to it."

By five o'clock, she could barely see the page. She was torn between a desperate longing to see Andy, a conviction that if she just stayed where she was long enough Andy would have to come, and the urge to sleep. If she got on the bus, she could lay her head back—it felt so heavy.

At five minutes to six, she dragged herself off to the phone. Standing up was becoming more difficult.

"Rest, Bad. Take the bus. Go home. I can't see you."

"Please, baby. I love you. I'm asking just one more time—won't you please see me for a while today?"

"Go home, Bad."

"Okay, I guess I will. Maybe I'm making a mistake, but I'm so tired."

Getting back on the bus was horrible. She was defeated. Her whole body ached, not just from fatigue. She leaned back into the seat and cried silently.

The ride back to Washington was horrible. The world was full of filling stations and lots of abandoned cars—all symbols of the emptiness and ugliness of life without Andy. Andy might be gone forever.

Going back to find a possibly enraged Ted was not particularly appealing, either, but it was nothing compared to this devastation. She was always going to be as alone and gray as this highway. She slept for about half an hour, then cried again. Her head throbbed.

She took a cab home from the station and lay on the bed. Thank goodness Ted was out, probably walking on the canal, or buying camping supplies.

Her exhaustion hung around her like a dark curtain, too painful to let her sleep.

She alternated between sleeping and crying, afraid. Ted came home, his bike by his side. She staggered to the living room to greet him.

"You saw the note?" She assumed that she had to make some reference to it.

His tone was as stiff and detached as possible. "I saw it. I didn't expect to see you here."

"She wouldn't see me. But I love her—it'll all work out, I know it will. I was up all night at the bus station." She was ashamed for him to know about the problems, but didn't know how to conceal them.

"Hmmm," he said, speculatively and not enthusiastically.

"Excuse me, I'm so tired. I don't much want to talk, but of course I will if you want."

"No, I don't want to talk. I'm going to Hechinger's to buy tools to fix my bike. The axle's loose."

For once she was relieved that Ted never wanted to talk about "heavy" things. It was awful to see his iron-jawed determination to stay married to her no matter what, and more awful to see his bitterness expressed in silence rather than tears.

On Sunday morning the phone rang. Brenda lunged at it, and found that it was Andy.

"Hello. How are you doing?" Andy's voice was positively sheepish. "I guess I'm feeling a little guilty for making you go home after you waited all that time."

"I'll come now, today, if you want."

"No, no, hold on there. I didn't mean that. I just feel bad that you went to all that trouble."

"Does that mean, by any chance, that I am forgiven?"

"I guess so. Maybe I'm the one that needs forgiving—or a good swift kick—for treating you like that."

"No, no, everything's fine if we make up."

Andy would not talk long on the phone and was still a little reserved.

On Tuesday a letter arrived that said,

Darling Bad,

It breaks my heart to say this, but I have to break up with you. I feel so guilty about how I've treated you, and you've been so good and understanding. I hate myself for letting you stay at the bus station—I could have hitchhiked into town—and making you go away.

Bad, I think I'm going crazy. I'm just not acting the way I used to. I keep having strange thoughts. Go away, honey, stay away from me. I'm no good for you. It may kill me to give you up, but I know I have to.

Don't be too angry at me. I do appreciate all you have done. Maybe you'll remember me sometimes. I know I'll always love you.

Love,
Andy

Brenda practically ran to the nearest phone.

"Andy, what do you mean? I can't break up with you, silly. You're perfectly fine as far as I'm concerned. The bus station incident was okay, I'd hurt you—we'll laugh about it someday."

"I don't think it's very funny, Bad." Andy's voice was glum.

"Oh, of course it is, just a funny little anecdote—it's all over."

"No, it's not. I'm afraid I'm a little crazy."

"Good, so am I. So's everybody."

"No, not like that, Bad. More than everybody. I have to be crazy to be giving up a woman who's everything I ever wanted, don't I?"

"How true, how true," she tried to make her voice sound light. "If you do succeed in giving wonderful me up, it will be proof that you are indeed crazy. However, I do not intend to let that happen, so you will not be proved crazy."

"Bad, that's crazy."

"I know. I told you I was crazy too."

Waiting for Andy left Brenda suspended in time. She thought of nothing but letters and phone calls, remembering those that had been and rehearsing those yet to be. Thank goodness other things were routine, her work was fairly routine, taking the bus was routine. Picking up some food for dinner was routine—having dinner with Ted was, unfortunately, routine, a part of the routine that she would surely eliminate soon.

"Can you really love me that much? Wanting to be with me, even if I'm crazy?" Andy asked.

"Of course. You'd better want to be with me when I'm crazy too."

"Oh, I will. You go crazy, and I'll finally be sane and take care of you day after day."

"It's a deal. So I can come this weekend?"

"Never give up, do you? Yes, I guess you can come."

"Hooray," she yelled into the phone.

Andy broke up. "Well, I'm glad you're so pleased. Hooray, yourself."

10

When Brenda boarded the bus for Cleveland, she was filled with exaltation. Buses and bus stations were no longer menacing barriers, blocking her way, but channels to carry her triumphantly to Andy. The seediness once again became simplicity.

As she rode through D.C., past Scott Circle and out of the city on 16th Street, she made her decision. She was not completely unafraid. Getting to know Ted had been so easy—and he was present, so constantly, predictably present and ready to cook dinner, not always caring if it wasn't his turn, ready to go for a walk, ready to go to the movies—waiting for her in case she wanted to sleep with him again. Andy seemed to operate on some unpredictable schedule of her own.

Ted has had everything, she told herself. Family, education through the Ph.D., respect, fun—why shouldn't he be easy? No one has ever despised him or stood in his way. If I break his heart, it will be the first time that has happened to him

Even if choosing women over men means choosing "sickness" over "health," "weakness" over "strength," pain over comfort, I choose women—forever, again and again, I shall choose women. The "sickness" and "weakness" are not intrinsic, they have been instilled, force-fed. Choosing women is not necessarily easier, will not necessarily make me happier in every way, may make my life much more precarious. I value security—am desperate for it. I do not despise security, day-to-day reliable presence, at all. I need it. But I shall give up that, or anything, for women. For Andy. Because none of us will ever be stronger, less panicked, if we do not choose one another now.

And in the formerly ominous Cleveland station, there was Andy, in a pale pink suit, saying "Hi" shyly and not looking her in the eyes. Brenda wanted to sweep Andy into her arms then and there, but was afraid Andy would be embarrassed. After all, it was her city, so the degree of public affection must be her choice. How warm, how full of life the station was now.

They departed, more quietly than usual, for the hotel.

Once they were in the room, Brenda tried to embrace her. "Andy, I'm so happy."

Andy turned away and sat down on the bed. "Not yet. I can't stand it yet. I feel so guilty. I don't deserve to have you make love to me."

"Of course you deserve it. You're wonderful. I love you. I'm so sorry about everything. Don't worry—we don't have to make love. We'll just be together as we did on the first night, if that's what you want."

"I'm so glad you're here. I don't deserve you."

"Oh stop sayin' that."

As they undressed, Andy said, "It's my period."

"Ah ha! Well, I don't know if I can resist making love to you, then, my beauty. That's so sweet—I think menstruation is the dearest thing —it reminds me of Louisa May Alcott —when I was an adolescent, I always read Louisa May Alcott books during my period. I must warn you that I love the smell of menstrual blood." She stroked Andy's upper leg.

Andy looked wicked. "No, now Bad, hold back—not 'til tomorrow."

"Foiled again! Oh, you wear kotex!" The white belt and cotton pad looked so touching on Andy's body.

"Always have."

"Really! Me, too. I don't like having things inside me—have only tried tampax a few times, and it hurt. I suppose I'd get used to it, but I love the sight and smell of my blood; I'd miss it."

"I like it, too."

"How lesbian of you."

"You're pretty lesbian yourself."

"Let me change your kotex." She reached over to touch it.

"Oh, Bad, you're too much." She stopped Brenda's hand, but they kissed.

"How are your cramps?" Brenda asked, stroking Andy's stomach.

"Not too bad. They couldn't be bad at all with you around."

In the morning, they made love and she tasted the new flavor. "A new sauce on the oyster, my dear. Wonderful. But you don't need a kotex—we can just leave my hand there all the time. Wouldn't that be convenient?"

"Oh, yes, very. I can just see that. I can't wait to taste your menstrual blood."

"Maybe next week you can. Now wouldn't you like to come again, presh? A period is such a nice time to lie back and be passive."

"I'm afraid it is. Most of the time I like making love best, but during my period I like being made love to best."

"I'm just the same."

In the afternoon, Andy said that she wanted to go out for half an hour by herself.

"Can't I go with you? I'd love a walk too."

"No, young lady, you stay right here."

"You will return?"

"Oh, you nut—of course I'll return."

"You damn well better, or I'll search the city—forever." She caught her around the waist and kissed her.

"I'll be back."

Brenda tried to read. Walking seemed so infinitely appealing. Being in bed was beautiful, but couldn't they ever walk in a park, see a movie, or go to an art gallery? She began twitching and glancing at her watch every minute when the half hour had passed.

Andy returned in about an hour, looking shaky.

"Is anything the matter?"

"I'm just tireder than I thought—that's all. Look, honey, I brought you a birthday present. I know it's early, but I wanted to give it to you anyway. I have some weekend seminars coming up at work, so maybe I won't be able to see you then, anyway." Brenda's birthday was going to arrive in two weeks—but the announcement that she might not be with Andy on the day took most of the pleasure out of the present.

Two packages were handed to her. "Two? Thanks, honey."

The first held a fluffy white toy kitten. "Isn't it cute?"

"I tried to get a black one, but I couldn't find it."

"What a pit—white will have to do. Well, she wants to be black, I'm sure—we'll call her after you anyway. Andette—is it okay?"

Andy laughed. "Andette, that's fine."

The other package was smaller—for some reason, she hoped that it contained a ring. But the gift was a gold locket with a representation of Virgo, her astrological symbol, on it. She did not like jewelry with astrological symbols, although she had always enjoyed the idea that she was a "Virgo." She was disappointed that they didn't have the same taste in jewelry—although she was ashamed of herself for having such a petty thought. "It's lovely."

"Turn it over."

The back of the locket said, "Andy Loves Bad." To Brenda, this seemed a touching simplicity. She would never have had such a message engraved on a piece of jewelry. How obnoxious I am, she thought. I must appreciate this better. " 'Andy loves Bad'—how sweet. I hope so. Andy better, or Bad will be very upset." She put the chain around her neck.

"I bought it yesterday but had to leave it overnight to be engraved. Someday I'll give you a ring, but I don't dare yet."

"Thank you. I hope you will." Crazy how much she cared about such an old-fashioned item, so discredited by its connection with patriarchy. They kissed, but it was evident that Andy wasn't very well. She lay down for a while, and Brenda, after some anxious questions about her health, followed by reassurances by Andy, went to a chair to read again.

I wish she were healthy and we could go out and do something. How awful I am—maybe she's really very ill—maybe it's the blood clot—but I'd rather have had an afternoon walk together than this locket.

So they continued living by the rhythm of the hotel, keeping a permanent "Do not disturb" sign on their door, leaving for lunch so that the maid would have a chance to enter the room. They always messed up both double beds, just in case someone in the hotel would make trouble. They ate the latest possible dinner in the red and black hotel dining room, staring deep into one another's eyes.

Again, Brenda begged to be allowed to stay beyond the weekend, and again Andy insisted that she go. Andy never did get completely well, but perhaps it was just the period.

This weekend had been "layout weekend" at the newspaper, the time when articles were typed and arranged on the graph board they later took to the printer to be photographed and offset. It was the first layout Brenda had missed in two years; if she returned on Monday, she could work on the final evening before the Tuesday printer date. She had told Andy, so of course Andy insisted that she return.

Layout was an ordeal. Many women stayed up all night to finish their work. Some did not finish writing their articles until the last minute, then asked for help in laying them out. Brenda was the sort who finished her own work early and was somewhat self-righteously annoyed at always helping the same last-minute people every month. Her layout work was not particularly adept—her letter-pressed headlines (made by rubbing a stencil-like page with a stick of wood) often had broken letters, and she was not good at aligning her articles in straight lines. She had been impatient with the work, as with all work with her hands (except cooking), wanting it to be done immediately. After two years, she was just barely getting the hang of it.

Layout was more than a time for work—it was also rather a social session. There was flashy repartee, occasional affection and/or flirting, an ocean of tense undercurrents. Some women on the paper were each other's lovers, and these giggled, snuggled, and teased one another occasionally, or one would do the other's letter press. Some were ex-lovers, and these passed one another with occasional tenderness, occasional aloofness or abrasion. Women went out to dinner together in groups or in couples.

The group dinners used to be more frequent. Brenda, for one, had been thrilled at first by the camaraderie, but soon felt unable to sustain her own brand of communication well in a group. Several women were much quicker-witted—and large groups, even of feminists, were not likely to engage in the lengthy soul-unburdening or abstract conversations she knew. She also made rather more references to her cat than good taste allowed, and her obviously tense reaction to drinking—she never had more than one drink herself and had trouble hiding her discomfort when others had many—did not make her the liveliest of companions. She was considered a positive teetotaler.

Layout was a humorous occasion—when she was able to be funny, she enjoyed it; when she wasn't, she felt like a dark mole, toiling in the midst of an uproarious party; she tried putting on blinders, so that she didn't see what was happening around her. She was so afraid of saying the wrong thing—and an unfunny joke is about as wrong as you can get—that she preferred to be silent.

There were likely to be political disagreements at layout, also, which added to the tension. Since theirs was a political newspaper, and since they usually saw each other's articles for the first time at layout, there were frequent debates about the political correctness of a particular article or statement.

Brenda had secretly longed to have a lover there near her at layout—perhaps everyone who had not yet had the experience longed for it; not to help her with the work itself—indeed, it made her nervous to have anybody help her—but for presence. It was a dreadful, unfeminist rejection of autonomy, no doubt, but she felt an almost physical desire to have a person there who was particularly connected to her. Being with Ted had shown how secure it felt to go places as a couple, to be able to turn to one other person in a room and feel understanding. Of course, she had friends, but that wasn't the same thing, especially since Nina had her lover Margo with her and Dolly had a male lover and usually left layout early to be with him.

Now that Andy existed, Brenda longed to have Andy walk through the doors of the office and be there with them, part of her life. She missed Andy—how stupid it had been to leave her, how stupid it was to live in different cities. She wore the new chain around her neck, hoping someone would ask about it. Nicole did, was shown the inscription, and teased her kindly. "Andy is wonderful," Brenda confided to a number of women.

The phone rang all evening, as it usually did during layout. One time it was for her.

"Hello, honey," purred a soft voice. "Who's laying you out? May I interrupt?"

"I'm so glad you called. Thank you, thank you. We don't lay each other out, silly, we lay the paper out."

"I'm jealous."

"Don't be. There isn't anybody in the world you should be jealous of—except maybe my cat."

"I am, I am. Lucky cat. But I'm jealous of the paper, too. I miss you."

Brenda was so happy that she started telling other women on the paper, even those who were not close friends, that Andy was going to move to D.C. eventually and they would live together. She said this not only because of her joy in Andy but because of her desire to show that she really was going to leave Ted. Maybe it would all happen by January.

11

A letter arrived.

Dear Bad,

Life is so strange that I don't know what to make of it. You have been so good to me and I've been very happy. I never dreamed that I could meet another woman who could interest me.

There is a new woman in my office named Eileen. She is a radical lawyer, and I really like how she treats the people who come in, with respect. I didn't know she was gay and she didn't know I was.

After you and I started going together, I started wearing my women-symbol chain, that I hadn't worn since Maxy's death. Eileen noticed it right away and started talking to me more and asking me out. I told her about you, but she kept on anyway.

This week, when I've been home sick, she's been coming to visit me every day. She took me to the doctor's and has helped me a lot.

She has told me that she loves me and will take care of me. I think I really care about her. I don't know what to do. She has shown that she cares.

Our being in different cities makes it so hard, Bad. We can't keep on meeting in hotels—I'm not a millionaire.

Eileen and I both do the same kind of work, so we can understand each other. You are a writer—that's different. Maybe you'll want another writer someday.

I do love you, but I think I love Eileen, too. But I'm monogamous—-that's the only way I can be. I have to choose. Even if I choose her, I want you to know how grateful I am to you for all that you have done. Eileen says that she is grateful to you, too, for helping me. You have saved my life, and I can never forget that.

Please don't be angry at me, Bad. I'm trying to do what is best.

Love,
Andy

The sentences in the letter struck Brenda like a series of blows that shook her body. She sobbed violently.

This time Andy's placating expressions held very little weight. Brenda was in a rage, not placated at all. She tried to call Andy, but there was no answer.

She sat down and, with trembling hand, wrote:

Dear Andy,

I never would have believed that you could do such a thing. I have loved you and trusted you more than anyone else in my life. Perhaps I've been foolish.

I am angry. I feel cynical. Of course I always knew that there was an arbitrary element in any two people getting together, but there is no need to play up that arbitrary element, surely, once two women are together.

I have been completely serious with you, given my life to you, and you—what are you doing? You say I saved you. So what if I did? That isn't the point, that isn't why I love you and I didn't think that was why you loved me. I wanted to put that part of our lives behind us. What are you trying to do, destroy me? You make me want to run in front of a car myself. Oh don't worry, I won't do it.

How could you do this to our love, our dear, tender, romantic, precious love? Damnit, our love is sacred. How could you consider breaking it off so soon, not giving it a chance? I could tear you limb from limb. Not literally, of course.

As for that woman—well, I won't say much of what I think about anybody who would do such a thing. Let her find someone else.

But the main point of this is not my anger—the point is that I love you, love you desperately. You can't imagine that I won't fight to keep you—of course I shall. What difference does it make who lives where if we love each other? I'll move to Cleveland the moment you tell me to. Of course someone who is near you can help more when you are ill, but I have offered, time and time again, to stay, and you refused me. How dare you punish me for not staying when you wouldn't let me stay! You know I want to be with you all of the time. Of course we can't keep meeting in hotels—I don't have much money either. Let's get a cheap place together in Cleveland.

Understand that I'm angry precisely because I love you so much. I can't bear to lose you. We've been so happy together. Precious baby, please, please don't give up this wonderful love.

Your own,
Bad

She hurried out and mailed the letter.

Later that day, she reached Andy.

"Oh hello, did you get my letter?" Andy sounded as if she was trying to be cheerful but the cheer didn't work.

"Yes." Brenda struggled to control her tone. "I was pretty upset."

"I'm sure you were." The tone seemed intended to be soothing.

"If you want to know the truth, I'm angry." Careful, be careful, she told herself. Don't let her think you don't love her. Don't *say* anything about that damn woman who's trying to throw herself in our bed, between us.

"I'll bet you are," Andy chuckled slightly. "I can just picture you angry." Her tone became more dejected. "I don't know how to explain this, Bad. Nothing like this has ever happened to me before —I've always been faithful to other women I've been with."

"Great. I'm the first. That makes me feel just great."

"I know it makes you feel bad. But it makes me wonder—nothing like this has happened to me before, so maybe it means there's something wrong with us."

"Maybe it's not us. Maybe it's all the other things you've been through recently."

"Maybe."

"Oh damnit, I love you, I love you, I love you. I need you. We've been so happy together. Let me come back to Cleveland—how can you complain about my not being there when you send me away? I'll come back and do anything anyone else would do for you—and more."

"Not *now*, Bad! You couldn't come here *now*! That would be a mess."

"I don't give a damn how messy it would be. Let me meet this Eileen. I'll appeal to her, compete with her, fight with her—anything."

"No! Don't you do any such thing! She's friendly toward you, she says."

"I'll bet, very."

"I don't expect you to like her. That's asking too much."

"Can't you wait some more time, think more before getting involved with her?"

"I *am* trying to do that, Bad, but she's pushing awfully hard."

So what, damnit, don't you have a mind of your own, she thought. Aloud, she said, "I'm sure she is, honey, but do you have to listen? Do you have to take her so seriously? If you do love me, can't you wait?"

"I do love you, Bad."

Andy's soft voice gave Brenda the usual thrill.

"I know, baby, and I love you. Please, dearest, let's work on that."

"You still love me? Even with all this?"

"Of course I do. I'd love you despite a thousand Eileens."

"Oh, Bad, that's awful. You shouldn't. A thousand. What do you think I'm like?"

"I think you're a dear, wonderful woman who is going through a rough time." And who drives me crazy.

Brenda felt so much pain that it frightened her. Something sharp seemed to keep going through her chest. Her appetite was gone. When she walked across an intersection, she felt almost compelled to throw herself under a car's wheels. The words "she's throwing herself in our bed" kept pounding in her head, she so wanted to scream them.

The happiness had not lasted long enough. Couldn't she have more than a few weeks of happiness?

Nothing in life seemed pleasant. The sunlight was an insult. She didn't want to see anyone—she desperately wanted to see friends and confide in them. She was humiliated that she had told everyone about Andy, had been so certain of the relationship, and now there was no one there, no wonderful lover to produce, to move in with her.

At noon on Brenda's birthday Andy called. "Well, I guess I ought to tell you that I came to a decision."

"Yes." Brenda's body tensed into total attention.

"I guess it's Eileen."

"I thought it would be."

"I know it's hard for you. I don't expect you to forgive me."

"Of course I forgive you. I love you anyway. I'll love you just as much." She must get the words in. Maybe there would be another chance someday.

"No, you won't. You couldn't love me if I slept with her."

"Yes. I could. I want to keep in touch with you despite all of this, okay?"

"If you really want to. I can't believe you do."

"Of course I do."

"Well, I guess I'd better get off the phone. Can't say too much to you after that. Good-bye, Bad."

"Good-bye, Andy."

Her body shook and ached—she hugged herself, literally trying to hold herself together. It was over—Andy would be somebody else's lover. They might never see each other again. Stuffing her face into a pillow, Brenda screamed.

The world was a frightening place, where lovers could be parted easily and no one was safe.

Brenda waited a few days—to give Andy time to sleep with

Eileen, and then set out to call to prove her love. (If she called the very next morning, perhaps right after Andy got out of bed, it might be too hard on Andy.) Hands trembling, but feeling a surge of strength, she dialed Andy's work phone number.

"I just wanted to call. Hope you don't mind."

"No, indeed."

"Things are rather rough here—I'm not getting too much work done this week. Of course, I am billing bookstores, which is a bit of a pain. I just thought I'd tell you that I love you."

"I guess you do." Andy's voice was strong with confirmation.

"Well, of course, silly."

"You're the silly one. A lot sillier than I ever imagined. Are you taking care of yourself, Bad? Have you been sleeping?"

Brenda almost cried with delight at hearing the warmth in Andy's tone. She wanted any crumb that she could get. "Certainly—several minutes a night."

"Bad! That's terrible! You need sleep. So you called today anyway." Andy seemed to be putting much tenderness in her voice.

"I just want to hear your voice."

"You still want to hear my voice. Bad, you are something else. Maybe I'll tell you something. You think I've slept with her, but I haven't—I couldn't. She isn't too pleased. I haven't changed my decision, but I haven't been able to do that."

"I love you." She was floating. Her fight might be doing some good after all.

"It may sound crazy, but I love you, too. I shouldn't say it, I know, because I don't know how much I'm going to do for you."

"Hearing it is good anyway."

So they continued to talk every day.

Of course, I know how ironic that is, she told herself. Andy's turning the tables on me, making me the desperate woman on the end of the phone, begging for sympathy. Maybe she's trying to destroy me—what a horrible person I am to have such thoughts. Of course she wouldn't do that deliberately—at least not consciously. What right do I have to read unconscious motives into her?

"I don't want to do anything but love anymore. What does my work mean if I can't be with Andy? It seems flat. Have I gone deeper, beyond it, or am I being shallow or hysterical to be so concerned about love, to the exclusion of everything else?" she asked Dolly.

"I don't believe in that kind of love," Dolly said, as if love were a slightly shady practice, like fortune-telling or gambling. "I don't believe in romance. Romance just hurts people. I gave it up years ago. Women have spent too much time on love. You just meet somebody casually, and if you get along, you get along." Dolly had lived with the same man for five years.

"No, no, that's not me. I can't be that way. That sounds feminist, I suppose. I know it isn't politically correct to believe in romance, that romance supposedly differs from day-to-day living with a person—but I don't think it does differ, for me. I don't think I could live happily day-to-day with a person I wasn't romantic about or had never been romantic about. Of course I worry about what will happen to the feminist movement if we all become romantic fools, but I am a romantic fool, anyway. Maybe that's why I became a lesbian and you didn't. I hope that being in love with a woman will somehow make all this frenzy politically constructive, but I don't know how."

"You're a love junkie. It isn't helping you. There are so many other important things in your life." Dolly was almost pleading — her usual tone when she tried to convince friends of things for their own good. "Try not to concentrate on Andy. Maybe it'll work out someday, but you have to think of other things."

"You don't understand. Maybe you can't. Of course I need other things. Of course I love writing, the paper, my friends. But love with a woman is something I have needed for a long time, and haven't had enough of. I've put so much time and energy into other feminist things—I need a chance for this, to really be intimate with a woman. At last, I've found a woman I could love, a woman who could love me. How can I give that up easily? I feel desperate. I'm tired of being the work horse of the movement, of processing subscriptions, going to meetings, and even of writing articles while other women have the love affairs. I want Andy. I love Andy."

"I know you do. Andy knows you do. You're being good and patient with her."

"I don't know how good I am. I just want her so much. Maybe I'd be angrier if I didn't need her so much."

"Being patient is a more effective way of keeping her."

"I know, but I'm so tired of having to think about love strategically. I don't want to be like that. I want to be able to love, be open and say everything I think."

Dolly's lecturing became even more earnest. "You can't do that, Brenda Anne. You've got to stop telling people everything you think. People like a little mystery . . ."

"I don't. I like openness."

"Well, everybody else likes mystery. You can't go through life being the only person with all your cards on the table. Everybody else keeps a few in her hand."

"I know—I just want to end all that. To say everything, even the sillier things—oh, this is all so abstract, I just want Andy. That's why she's better than other women I've met, because I can be more open with her. I can be more of my real self—don't you understand?"

"I know you love her. But it won't do Andy any good to have you all torn up inside. Try to take care of yourself."

Reluctantly, she let Dolly go back to work.

In a few days, Andy reported that she had broken up with Eileen. Brenda and Andy made up, and Brenda resumed studying, an activity that had been suspended.

She arrived home with the latest stack of books. When she opened her mailbox, she saw that the telephone bill had arrived. Brenda repressed a shudder, as if she had received a letter bearing bad news. She carried it upstairs to her apartment and forced herself to open it. Two hundred and eighty-seven dollars. Well, getting Andy back from Eileen was worth it, even though it wiped out a quarter of her savings. She mustn't begrudge it. As long as she made sure that Ted never saw the bill, everything would be all right.

Andy called, and soon began making self-disparaging comments.

"Stop running yourself down. I don't listen to anyone who's running my Andy down."

"Your Andy ought to be run down—maybe with a car. Bad, you don't know the thoughts I've been having."

Her voice was so serious that Brenda began feeling frightened. Oh, no, not again. "What thoughts, presh?"

"I just keep remembering the hospital—everything that happened. Sometimes I almost see it in front of me—it's scary. I feel like I'm going crazy. I get the most horrible nightmares—I won't want to sleep because I'm frightened."

"Oh, Andy. You've been through so much. I'm sorry it's that bad. Maybe if we're together it'll get better. I want to be there with you."

"I don't know if it would be better. That's what frightens me. It doesn't make any sense. It happens when I'm thinking about lesbian things. Not about you—it hasn't happened when I think about you. But sometimes I'll look at a picture of two women together and I'll get this horrible feeling—a pain. I remember the shocks just like I was there. It scares me so much sometimes I think I'd do anything to get away from it. Sometimes I think I'd even go to a priest or a man or something to get away from it. I know that's a horrible thing to say when I have you, but I feel that way sometimes. And then guilty. That's why I couldn't get together with Eileen—not just because I felt guilty about you, but because I had those other feelings, too."

Brenda's skin crawled. She wanted to hide. A man! Nothing Andy had ever said before had made this sound possible. At least Eileen was a woman. The shocks couldn't make a person do that. She didn't know whether she was more upset about Andy's pain or about what Andy's pain might push her to do.

"I didn't know it was that bad. Poor Andy."

"Today I walked by a Catholic church and I almost went in to talk to the priest."

"Oh, no, you know what he'll say! 'Lesbianism's a sin, the shocks were bad but "curing" your lesbianism is good. Pray to the Blessed Virgin for purity, my child. Go your way and sin no more.' "

"Yeah, that's about it. I know. But where else can I go?"

"I hate to say it, but what about a therapist? I don't trust most of them but . . . "

"A shrink? That's how I got here in the first place."

"I know. But what else is there? Some of them are supposedly feminist now. There must be a feminist therapist somewhere in Cleveland. If not, there are some here."

"I get so frightened that I feel like I'd do anything to get away from it. I remember this man I went out with before I knew Maxy — his name's Al—and I wonder if going to him would get these things out of my head. Don't get upset, I won't do it."

"I hope not." She tried not to say too much. "Surely there are other things that can be done. I wouldn't be too thrilled about that alternative."

"I know, Bad. I want us to be together. Nobody knows better than I do how hard something like that would be for you. I wish I could get a lobotomy, get this cut out of me. I just want to stop feeling crazy."

"Get a lobotomy and you'll stop feeling anything."

"Right now, that doesn't sound so bad. Maybe I'll go commit myself somewhere."

"Jesus Christ, not an institution. That's how all this happened in the first place. How do you know they wouldn't shock you again?"

"I couldn't stand that. If they'd just agree not to do that, they could do anything else."

"Why the hell would you let them do anything? Why put yourself in their power? You can't commit yourself, you can't get a lobotomy—then you'd just be their puppet to use as they pleased." She didn't keep the anger out of her voice.

"Then nothing would be my fault anymore. Maybe I wouldn't feel so guilty about you then."

"Oh God, do I make you feel that guilty? Don't feel guilty, please don't feel guilty. If you committed yourself, what happened to you would be partly your fault and you know it. Can't you just find out if there's a feminist, gay, or pro-gay therapist around and have some sessions with her? You don't have to put yourself in somebody's power."

"I'll try. But they'd better be able to get rid of it quick. I can't stand it."

Brenda was trembling violently when she put down the phone.

The trouble was inside Andy, not just in the outside world of predators eager to seize her for their own ends. Something had been implanted in her brain. It was science fiction.

They couldn't turn a lesbian into a heterosexual just by a *machine*. That would make her a machine, too. If Andy accepts their message, that will mean that she's become a robot, Brenda thought. She can't let herself become a goddamn robot. They can't take my lover away with a machine. That *is* unnatural—screwing someone because a machine tries to make you.

Brenda wanted to shriek. Who the hell is this man, Al? The one she mentioned in the July letter about her life—who wanted to marry her? He can't still be around?

I'm sick and tired of having to be so goddamn reassuring. This is more than I can stand. She won't let me have one day, not even one day, to study in peace. She's going to destroy me. I'll lose the Ph.D. because of her. The Ph.D.? I'll lose my mind, maybe my life. Either we wind up together or it's all over for me. She can't do this to me. She can't betray me to men, priests, surgeons. I won't let her have a lobotomy. I won't let her be their puppet. I'll kill them. If any man comes near her, I'll kill him—or myself—oh God, which will it be? What *would* I do?

What she did do was grab a pen and paper, her usual solution to problems.

My Precious Andy,
    Please do tell me everything. I want to know what you suffer, to suffer what you suffer. I can't bear for you to be alone. You are not alone—you are part of me and I am part of you.

It is because of this union between us that I cannot bear the thought that you would ever go to a man. You are my heart, my body, my soul, and I do not want to give my heart, my body, my soul to a man ever again. I know that you are going through great torment, but please do not let them do that to you. It would be too ironic. *Men* are the ones who have tortured you, have made you suffer. You must not let them conquer you, must not let them see that they can get us by torture, or they will torture us all. Surely they cannot capture your soul. Even if they make it painful for you to think of women, how can they make you turn on to men? You can't let your sexuality be determined by a damned machine.

If any man ever, perish forbid the horrible thought, sleeps with you, he is attacking me. No matter how "nice" he may be, no matter whether he knows of my existence or not, he is my deadly enemy.

I cannot believe that the drama of our love could have the same ridiculous old ending as the classic lesbian love story—a man. That couldn't happen to us—not in this day and age. I'm sorry, but that just won't do as an ending.

Forgive me for this hysteria—I truly do feel hysterical, feel pain in my womb, everywhere. I love you so. I'll do anything I can. There is an old-fashioned saying that I've heard, "If you love me as I love you, then nothing but death can part us two." That's true, Andylove.

Your love, always,
Bad

12

The next day, they talked again about the therapist.

Andy said, "I went to a shrink. I got her name from a psychology student. She's even a lesbian—can you believe it?" Andy was ambivalent. "Sometimes it seems like so much trouble that I just wish I could forget sexuality altogether and not ever think about it again."

Brenda shuddered. "I suppose I should understand your feeling that way—but I wish you wouldn't. I must admit that I am very fond of your sexuality."

"Aw. I know, Bad. I know, honey. That's why it matters. I've buried a lot of what happened during the shock treatments: I don't remember it. Shirl says that I need to remember it so I can deal with it. She says that one way of curing people who've had shocks or other horrible experiences they can't remember is by hypnotizing them so they can remember. The problem is that they have to relive it, as if it was happening all over again. I'm scared to do that—once was bad enough. Ugh."

"Oh God, you'd have to live through it again? How horrible. How could I ask you to do that?" The horrible thing was that she did want to ask her to do it.

"Pretty freaky, isn't it? The worst part is that she can't even guarantee that it would work. It might help, it might do just the opposite. It might reinforce the conditioning and make me worse. I don't know—I love you, I want to do the right thing, but it scares me. The thought of going through all that and it just making things worse—I don't know."

Brenda made dark, slashing marks on her desk with a pen. "It's not fair that the burden should all fall on you. I wish I could share it more. I don't want you to go through that again. Isn't there something I can do? I want to be with you."

"That's the *problem*, honey. My being afraid to be with you. It's all a delayed reaction to the shocks, Shirl says. That's why I keep running from you even though I love you. That awful night when you waited at the Greyhound station was the first time. Eileen was the same thing."

"But it was so good when we were together. It was beautiful. That was after the shocks."

"I know. It was a *delayed* reaction. I don't want to feel the pain when I think of you. I haven't yet, but I'm afraid I will. She explained that's why I'm staying away. She does think it would be bad if I felt the pain when we were together. She says it's better for us to be in different cities. She said maybe if we were in the same city, she'd ask us not to see each other for a while anyway, so I don't associate you with the pain."

"Well, for heaven's sake don't tell her about the letter in which I said I'd kill myself if you went straight. I don't think a shrink would like a thing like that."

Andy chuckled. "That was a fine, angry letter. Don't worry, Bad. I wouldn't tell a shrink anything like that. I know you can't tell shrinks everything."

It's clear, it's clearer, Brenda Anne said to herself. Clear as barbed wire. Andy's afraid to see me. Me. I never hurt her. I could never hurt her. They did it. The doctor ought to die—I hope he gets shocked by one of his own machines—let his machines stop him from sleeping with women. Castrate the bastard.

He castrated her—castrated my Andy. Tried to. No man was ever more castrated than she is—can't even think—

So brave—not crazy. They're wrong—she's the strongest. But if it was me, I'd see my lover. I would. I would.

I wouldn't hurt her—I'd rather die than hurt her.

But if I want her to go through the hypnosis, if I let her go through it, then I *would* be willing for her to be hurt. I would be hurting her—I would be guilty. I can't stand it—it's too horrible.

Her politics had told her that this sort of horror was possible, but she hadn't believed it in her gut.

Andy went to the therapist every day, and they had a long phone conversation after her appointment.

"I'm amazed that your office lets you take all this time off. It's good that they do."

"Oh, they aren't any problem. Sometimes I say I'm going to the law library to look up things, or to the courthouse. They don't know the difference. I've been there a long time, they know me, so it's okay. It doesn't bother them—it bothers me. I used to care so much about my work, worry about every person who came in here. Now none of it matters—I can't think about anything but myself."

"I don't think that's so strange—there can't be many clients at the center whose problems are as heavy as yours. It won't last forever."

"How do you know it won't? It might—not everybody gets better. I think it must have been my fault in the first place—being suicidal—letting them get hold of me. Letting myself be so depressed about being gay. Shirl says the attitude you have when you go through the shocks makes a difference. The attitude I had was terrible. Somebody else might have been less susceptible—stronger. It is my fault."

"Don't worry about that now. You were strong. You were amazingly strong when you got out of the hospital."

"Yeah, amazingly. Amazing enough to get you tied to me. You poor thing."

"Oh, don't say that, nutsie. I want to be tied to you."

"Do you want me? Do you still really want me? Do you still feel romantic about me sometimes, despite everything?"

"Yes! Are you kidding? If you could just put your arms around me again, and hold me, as you did that first evening, I'd be so happy that I'd never complain again. I miss you so much."

"I miss you, too. I do want to put my arms around you, to kiss your lips very softly. I'm glad that you want me, too, so glad." Her voice trembled. "I didn't know whether you really wanted me romantically still, despite everything. I let myself think of you that way sometimes, but I get afraid—and so depressed when I think of never touching you again."

"Then don't think it. There's still hope if you can still feel attracted to me. Just hearing that makes me almost happy enough to cry. I could just hold you in my arms, brush back the curls on your forehead, and kiss every inch of your face. I'd nuzzle against your neck and sink my lips into it, while I let my hand start to stroke your left breast, very softly . . . " Her voice became throaty.

"Bad! Don't do that! You make me feel—" Andy sounded happier than Bad had heard her in months.

"That's the idea," Brenda purred, very consciously. "I want you to feel good and sexual—sexual and good. Shall we give it a try?"

"Over the phone? I don't know. I'm a little scared."

"I'll stop the minute you tell me to. Don't worry."

"I don't know if we should."

"Would Andy's soft breasts mind being touched? I don't want to do anything they'd mind. Maybe they'd rather I just sucked the nipples?"

"Bad! My goodness!" a jolly little prim voice said. "You're scandalous."

"Just relax, honey."

"Oh, you're so wicked that I'm just going to have to put down this phone."

"Yes, I am wicked, and I'll catch you in my spell, beauty."

"My goodness! What shall I do?"

Brenda was happy, positively happy.

On Saturday morning, Andy called. Ted was gone—Brenda was waiting, still in her long, flowered flannel nightgown.

"My grandmother has gone out shopping."

"Oh, how convenient. And where are you? Still in bed, I hope?"

"I shouldn't tell—yes."

"Mmm—wearing a nightgown?"

"Bad! Yes. A pink flannel nightgown."

"How sweet."

"Are you wearing a nightgown too?"

"Yes."

"And you're alone?"

"Definitely."

"I don't know about this."

"What don't you know, baby? Let me say hello to your whole body. Hello, Andy's toes. I haven't seen you in a long time. Let me kiss you. Hello, ankles—let's stroke you a little, with the tips of my fingers. I'll stroke the whole right leg, starting from the ankle, up to the—thigh."

"Oh, my goodness."

Her voice purred, deeply, like a tall actress, infinitely more worldly wise than Talullah Bankhead.

"I'm stroking near Andy's pretty fur—mmm, but not yet. Let me kiss you on the lips—softly, so softly." Her voice became almost inaudible. "Long, soft."

"Mmm, Bad." Andy sounded so good. Her voice lifted Brenda up, like a wave.

"I kiss you. Harder. Our tongues slide over each other. We're clasping each other—tightly. I hold you—tighter, tighter."

"I'm kissing you, Bad. I kiss *you.*" The voice shook with intensity.

"Darling. So wonderful. I kiss you—I kiss all around your mouth. I hold onto each bit of your lips, not wanting to let go."

"Ohhh. Bad."

"I'm kissing your shoulder now, moving my lips down to your left breast. I kiss the tip of the breast. You taste so good. Your breasts still taste different from the rest of your body."

"Bad." The voice choked, almost as if she were close to tears.

"Is it all right?"

"Oh, yes, Bad."

"My mouth moves around your nipple. My lips grasp you. My tongue rubs against the tip. I suck you."

"Bad, oh Bad."

"You taste so good, Andy." She made sucking sounds. The sight, the taste of Andy's body were overwhelmingly present. Her own body shook with excitement. She didn't touch herself—she didn't need to touch herself. Her body was filled with a feeling far more powerful than her own touches could ever bring.

"I'm sucking still. I move my hand down, stroking your sweet stomach. I touch your hair and rub softly the area under the hair. My mouth to your right breast. I kiss its soft sides. I lick the nipple, very lightly. I suck the nipple. I love you, Andy."

"I love you, too."

"I rub softly near your oyster. I touch it, Andy. I'm rubbing your oyster, trying to find just the right place."

Andy was breathing heavily.

"Are you all right?"

"Yes—oh yes."

"Are you really excited? That's so wonderful. Andy, you make me so happy. You excite me, too. Just listening to the wonderful sound of your breath. My whole body is shaking. I move down and lick your lovely oyster. You're so pretty. You taste so good. Oh Andy, I'm so happy." She spoke very slowly, pronouncing each word slower than the last. "I love you. Andy. Oh, you taste so good. Let me find the dearest spot—there. Andy. I love you so much, honey. Your breath is so wonderful. Oh. Please let me hear, Andy. Annndy. My lover. Baby. Andy."

"Oh. Ohh. Bad. Ohh, Bad. Ohh."

The beautiful sounds of Andy's murmur reached a crescendo. Brenda's head was dizzy. They were both in tears. The murmur subsided.

A moment later she dared to ask, "Andy? Did you come?"

"Yes, Bad. Oh." She could hardly talk.

"How wonderful." Brenda sobbed a little. She had never thought that she would be this happy again.

"Th-thank you, Bad."

"Don't thank me, thank you." Each sentence came from the depths of silence and subsided into a tranquil pause.

"I love you."

"I love you."

It was a little melancholy having her lover vanish when she hung up the phone, but Brenda did not let herself veer into melancholy. She lay there, her eyes half-shut, remembering each moment. She drank a long, slow Coca-Cola and wrote an affectionate message to Andy.

A few hours later, Andy called.

Brenda lifted the receiver reverently. Amazing the things you could communicate by telephone.

"I so happy!" Andy chirped. Brenda loved the way Andy dropped verbs when she chirped. "I always said your voice could make me do anything, but I didn't know you could do that."

"My innocent little voice? Why, what do you mean?"

"Innocent! Bad, if you dare talk to anybody else on the telephone, I'll cut the wires. I can't stand thinking about you answering the phone all day at the newspaper office."

"Oh Andy, it is going to work. We are going to be together always. We'll still be together in the old folks home."

"Yes. We'll be such sweet little old ladies together."

"There are so many things to look forward to! And I'd love to cook for you—what a shame I haven't had a chance to make some of my fabulous dishes—then you will be hooked forever. I'll bake you cakes—I'll make coq au vin, sauerbraten, my best Madras curry—and I hope you like Chinese food?"

"I love it."

"Of course there will also be all sorts of oysters—stuffed oysters, oysters cooked in various liquors . . . I'll give you the best-cooked oysters you've ever had."

"Oysters. That's all you think about."

"Sure. Oh, you make me feel so domestic."

"Oh yes, I know how domestic you are. I'll clean the house. I'll do the washing and ironing. I'll fix the plumbing . . . "

On Monday morning, Andy saw the therapist again, and then, of course, called.

"What did she say?" Brenda was anxious, afraid that the therapist might find something the matter with their new way of loving.

"Her name is Shirl. She said it was a very good sign, it's wonderful that we can do it. She said she'd been afraid that maybe I was just hanging on to you, that it wasn't still a living relationship, but now she's sure." Andy's voice became very quiet. "I'm going to have the hypnosis, Bad. I think it's the only chance."

Brenda couldn't deny that she was pleased, but she felt ashamed of herself as well as afraid. "Andy. Are you sure? You don't have to."

"Yes, I do, if I want us to be together again."

"Not to be melodramatic, but you know that I think you're the bravest person in the world, don't you?"

"Not so brave, honey."

Ted's presence had become more intolerable. She spoke to him less and less. She didn't even want to read in the same room: he was large and restless, always rattling his book, jumping up to make popcorn, crunching the popcorn, making a remark to an indifferent cat (really an excuse to talk to her), or exclaiming over his science fiction story. When he went in one room she would go in the other. She was pleased to see that the cat followed her.

Even Ted's smells permeated the small rooms. He was always smearing on some kind of after-shave lotion or salve to soothe his muscles from the latest hike. Sitting near him nauseated her. Walking past him almost overpowered her stomach. She tried not to let him see how nauseated she was—after all, he had been as good to her as he could have been.

How much things changed, she thought. She had once considered the sight of him in his blue velour bathrobe—an early present from her, because she thought velour was sexy—attractive. Now, the sight disgusted her. He would be naked under the bathrobe, and was always letting the bathrobe fall open.

"Can't you go out this evening?" she asked him. She didn't want him in the next room.

"This is my home. I don't have to go out."

"That's true. I was just asking."

She cleared her books to the bedroom to await Andy's call, and shut the door.

Staying with him made her feel guilty. But it was only ten days until exams, and the phone calls were draining her savings. The more intolerable staying was, the more impossible leaving seemed.

Andy called. Brenda settled in on the raggedy old sofa bed.

"Hello, you wicked woman."

"Aha, my pretty, alone together at last."

They made love over the phone again, trembling with happiness.

A long time later, Andy said, "I'm going to do my best for us, Bad. I'm going to have the hypnosis tomorrow. I'm so happy that I'm ready to face anything."

"Tomorrow? Isn't that awfully soon after all of this? I hope I haven't made a mistake." The image of Andy going down the next morning into a cave where she would re-experience electric shocks when she saw pictures of naked women or heard the word "lesbian" hit Brenda forcefully. They were both glowing and tingling from love—she couldn't let her lover be torn away from her into that horror.

Perhaps I should try harder to stop her—or will that backfire, make her nervous and prevent the hypnosis from going well? What do I do? Nobody ever prepared me for moral questions like this. "Do you let the person you love re-experience electric shock pain in order to bring you back together?" That wasn't in the Baltimore Catechism. Neither can I find the answer in Plato, Marx, Louisa May Alcott, or Dostoievsky. None of them imagined that such horrible problems existed. Goddamned fool Catholic crucifix-worshipping bitch—me—do I have to crucify my beloved in order to love her? And I always thought I was the one who was saving her—Hah. This event strips those pretensions bare. She is really the suffering one—and I, having fallen in love with her suffering, am now forced to watch and cause it. It wasn't bad enough that she's been crucified once—no, she will again and again, for me. I became an atheist too late—or failed to become one completely enough.

Brenda slept on the worn old sofa near the phone—closer to Andy—even though it was too small for her to move and the roaches sometimes ran across it. She had postponed sleeping there too long.

"What are you doing?" Ted asked harshly.

"Putting some sheets on this. I'm going to sleep here."

"I won't touch you—you don't have to worry."

"I have to sleep alone. I suppose you won't sleep here?"

"No way. You're being dumb. Nobody has to sleep there."

"I will."

"Suit yourself. Don't blame me if the roaches crawl over you."

"Thanks a lot."

"What do you expect me to say?"

"Nothing." She knew she ought to be sorry for him. He would be lonelier in the canopy bed than she was on the old couch.

Welcome back, old bed. It reminded her of her first year in Cambridge, 1970, alone with the bed and Mouse in a seedy room.

Mouse jumped on the bed, walked up to her face, mewed, and touched noses.

Welcome back, cat. You'll like it that there's no one in the bed but us. Welcome back to the one, irreducible twosome, Brenda and Mouse. I'll never leave you.

She stroked the cat's cheek. He purred and kneaded her chest. When he moved to settle down, he mewed a little, complaining because there was little room, but fitted himself into a long, narrow space beside her leg.

13

She would not study. She would not think of anything but Andy during the hours when Andy might be at the therapist's. She would sit on the old couch and wait. It was the least she could do.

She felt like everywoman, trapped on a couch, waiting for a warrior who went to risk death, not allowed to risk death, too.

Let me feel it myself, please—let me feel the pain all over my body, instead of her—Brenda invoked the eternal nothing.

I hate men. I hate what they've done to Andy. I hate the fact that most of them would believe that psychiatrist was doing her a favor. I hate the fact that they try to program women to love them, only them and not each other. But I don't hate individual men, except when they torture women. I hate the psychiatrist who shocks. I don't hate George McGovern. I don't hate Mao Tse-tung. I don't hate Chou En-lai. I don't hate Dostoievsky. I don't hate George Burns, or Jimmy Durante. I don't hate . . . please, don't let me hate too much. I don't think Andy hates as much as I do.

The gray-haired woman urged Andy to relax.

"Sure thing. I'm just going to relive the shocks. Why not relax?" The thought made her automatically clench her hands. She tried to unclench them. It didn't seem as if her muscles could ever relax again. "I'm not going to be able to sleep on this couch."

Shirley smiled reassuringly and kept saying soothing things. Andy felt herself slip into a kind of sleep.

"I'm going to take you someplace pleasant, to relax you more," she heard Shirley's voice say. "Think of a park, a park you went to with Maxy. You are having a quiet, pleasant walk in the park with Maxy."

It was summer. There were dahlias. There was the river. Maxy was joking about a couple they knew, a very tight couple.

Then it was an ordinary day at work. The office was packed with people, mostly elderly. Some of them were being thrown out of their apartment building.

She was strapped down. "Dirty nigger dyke bitch." The doctor's hand passed over her breast. She wanted to vomit. She tried to scream. The machine.

Later, she was walking in the park again, alone, looking at autumn leaves.

She was on Shirley's couch, waking up. Her body was covered with sweat.

"Are you all right?"

"I guess so."

"You screamed a lot."

She called Bad and told her about it as soon as she had recovered a bit.

The next day Brenda called Andy's office, again and again. She tried to study—her exam was only a week away. There was a little resentment within her because of the exam, which was so important to her, was so unimportant compared to what Andy was doing.

Finally, Andy answered the phone. "I'm here." The voice sounded as if it came from far away.

"I suppose you are, though you don't sound there."

"I almost wasn't here."

"Did anyone try to hurt you?"

"Yes—I tried to hurt myself. Didn't make it, though. I never tried to shoot a gun before—I didn't know how hard it was—the impact. I just hurt my hand."

"Andy! Oh my God, oh baby. Oh no, please. I love you so much."

"It's no use, Bad. The reactions from the hypnosis have been so scary. I can't stand anymore."

"Were they about me—did you feel the pain about me?"

"Let's just say I had some reactions that Shirl said weren't too encouraging."

"I thought it was a mistake having that damn hypnosis so soon after making love. My poor baby. Are you all right now?"

"I twisted my hand falling over when the gun went off, but I'm okay—that way. It's just so frightening. I don't know if I can take it—it's like hallucinations—I feel as if I was there—tied up—with the machine. I see the strangest scenes of women—Shirl says they gave me drugs, too, so it'll be harder to undo."

"Oh, baby. So much for you to take."

"I *can't* take it, Bad. That's what I'm trying to tell you. I want to kill myself—for real now. This is worse than anything. I can't trust myself. I can't work, I can't do anything. I never know when these flashes will come."

"Andy. I love you so much. Please try to hang in there. Maybe it'll get better."

"I don't know if I can stand going back to Shirl."

"Don't worry about it. Maybe you'll go back someday."

"Someday! I can't wait for someday. You can't wait for someday. This has to get done."

When Brenda put down the phone, half her hope was gone. Suicide. Again. It had come full circle.

At ten-thirty that night, Andy called again.

Ted was in the bathroom—there was just a thin wall and some roaches between the bedroom couch and the bathroom. Hoping to keep him from hearing, Brenda ran to shut the bathroom door.

"Are you okay?" she asked into the phone.

"Sure, very okay. There isn't any hope, Bad. I keep getting those flashes. I'm afraid to be hypnotized again."

"Of course you are. That's all right; you don't have to be."

"Yes, I do. Bad, I don't want any more pain. I just don't want any more pain."

"Of course you don't."

"I shouldn't say this to you. I feel rotten about saying this to you. I'm just afraid to go to sleep. I'm afraid to be alone."

"I don't want you to be alone, baby."

"But I can't be with you, either—I can't do you any good."

At this point, a damp, naked Ted holding a towel strode into the room. "I want to go to bed," he said as if claiming a throne.

"I need to talk longer." She was furious.

"Make it short." He strode away.

"Damn him, he wants to go to bed. I wish the phone was in the living room."

"I'll get off."

"No, don't you dare. Good grief, you're more important than anybody's sleep."

A few minutes later, Ted popped in again. "I'm going to bed now."

"Please. Andy is really down. I need to talk with her." The words may have been polite, but her tone wasn't.

"You've talked long enough. You can keep on talking, for all I care, but I'm going to bed." He thrust his naked body into the canopy bed and pulled up the covers.

"Can't I have any privacy?"

"No, it's my bedtime."

"I'll just keep on talking then—though I object to your staying."

"That's tough. You can't keep me out."

"Excuse me, Andy. Ted just came into the room—I guess you heard. He insists on going to bed, so I have to talk in front of him. I hope you don't mind."

"All I bring you is trouble. You don't have to keep listening to me."

"I want to."

"But someday you'll wear out. I'm wearing out."

"Of course you're tired."

"Today really scared me, Bad. It wasn't like any other time I tried to kill myself. I didn't get depressed and think about it—it just hit me, all of a sudden—out of nowhere I just got the idea that I had to kill myself as quickly as possible, and I ran to the closet to get my gun that I bought after I got out of the hospital, when I was afraid that they might try to take me back. It was weird."

"So you don't feel suicidal now?"

"Not very—just very down—well, a little like the suicidal times last spring. But this morning was so different."

"If only I could do more to help."

"Bad, your being so sweet makes me feel sad."

"Don't feel sad because of me. You're the very dearest baby in the whole wide world. I love every bit of you."

"You're saying that in front of him!"

"In front of anybody."

"You're the boldest thing I've ever heard. I could listen to you all night."

They made love over the phone that weekend, during the day-time. Returning to each other's voice-caresses after the pain of the week was a great relief. The suicide attempt changed something inside of Brenda. If ever that could recur, the chances of equality between them were being eaten away. Perhaps Andy would never recover entirely.

She was still committed—a woman with a grain of morality

would never consider leaving someone weaker than she was,
Brenda told herself. Andy was so charming, so soft, so full of wit
that she would love her even if Andy were screaming rejections at
her.

The lovemaking did make her hope, but she was sadder after
they hung up than she had been. She resented slightly the fact that
it was not more reciprocal. She felt aroused, teary, a little deserted.
But somehow relieved. If it could happen even after the hypnosis,
perhaps it could always happen. Andy would be restored from hell
back to earth, like Persephone. You do not abandon Persephone
merely because she has to descend to hell again—you cherish her
all the more for that reason.

14

Brenda's tests were scheduled for all day Thursday and Friday. On the second day, her exam would focus on Communist countries. On the days immediately before the exam, Andy called her briefly to cheer her on.

"You ought to spend your time studying, not talking."

"I just want to know how things are going—with Shirl, for instance. How are the sessions?"

"Bad subject."

"What's the matter?"

"Let's drop it. Let's just say I'm not going to see her anymore."

"Why not? What did she do? Did the sessions get more painful?"

"It was something she said. I don't want to talk about it."

"Andy, please, I want to know."

"Not now, honey. I'm fine. Really. We can talk after your exams."

At the exam answering the questions, thinking, was pleasant in itself, a true exercise of her mental limbs. Brenda was sorry when she was done.

She could actually do something besides writing love letters and coaxing over the telephone. She was something else besides a lover, although she certainly was that. How strange—her first thought when she became a budding feminist was that she must study for the Ph.D. she wanted—but becoming a lesbian had made that seem somehow trivial, as if all those articles about women wanting and needing to work were wrong and love was the most important thing after all.

The next day after Ted left for his usual Saturday morning hike,

Brenda called Andy.

"What happened between you and Shirl? Did she make a pass at you? Destroy your ego? Tell you I was a poor sick idiot?"

"None of that, Bad."

"It was about us, wasn't it?"

"Yes, baby, it was about us. But I don't intend to pay any attention to it. She doesn't understand. I don't want to see her anymore, and that's the end of it."

"What did she say?"

"She said that we should separate for a while. Don't worry, I won't do it."

Even though she was not completely surprised by the nature of the message, Brenda was shaken. Knowing that a blow is coming doesn't diminish its force. "Separate!" she shrieked. "How the hell could we be any more separate than we are now? We're hundreds of miles apart—we aren't supposed to see each other. What more does that woman want to do to us?"

"Don't worry, I told you I wouldn't do it. She said that we should stop talking on the phone and writing letters—take a break from each other while I'm having the treatment."

"God damn her! She has no right to play with our lives like that. What about me? I'm a person, a real, live human being who loves you. How could I bear not even talking to you? I know she believes in considering her patient first, but I'm a human being, too. Doesn't she have to have some concern about how her theories affect other people in her patients' lives? I need to stay in touch with you." She was shaking and crying.

"Bad, honey. You see why I didn't want to tell you. Of course it would hurt you. I couldn't stand it either. I never want to see her again."

They murmured a few reassurances back and forth. The words "I love you" were frequently stated.

Eventually, Brenda started thinking. "Andy, are you still having the pains, the flashes, the nightmares and all?"

Andy made a sound that was a cross between a grunt and a groan, with a bit of a sick snicker thrown in. "Oh, they're all present and accounted for."

"You really do need a therapist to try to undo the damage done by the shocks. And Shirl knows you—and is supposedly a lesbian feminist—and apparently cares about you even if she's wrong about this. Maybe you should go back to her."

"How can you say that? I won't. You don't want me to give you up, do you?"

"No, of course not, but she can't force you to do that. I don't think there's much choice, baby, unless you want to look for another therapist."

"Oh, no, not another one. I've had it with them all. I don't know what I'll do—but not that. Maybe I'll go to some other city—and find a therapist. Or just fade into the crowd. Stop hoping—nothing's going to happen—she isn't curing me. Maybe I'm not going to be cured."

"I still think you should go back. I hope I'm not cutting my own throat by saying so."

"I don't know. Maybe I'll go back. I don't know what to do."

"Think about it, baby, that's all."

"I love you."

"Of course you do, and I love you, too. Your big brown eyes, whose eyelids I want to kiss . . . " She moved into her sultriest voice.

"Not now, Bad."

"No romance?"

"No way, honey. Not today. I think I'll go out or something. Bye-bye."

"Good-bye for the moment, my love."

Brenda had thought that making love over the phone was lonely. The fear that they would never do it again was much worse. "I can't even touch her with my voice," she thought.

Two days later, the phone rang.

"Andy!" Brenda exclaimed, leaping at the phone.

"Hello, honey. I just want to let you know that I did go back to Shirl."

"Good. I guess I'm glad. You'll note the hesitation in my voice. I hope she'll help."

"I don't know. I'm going to try. I've made a decision. Things can't go on like this forever. We're spending every cent we have on phone calls. You're tied down, waiting for me . . . "

"I want to wait!"

"It's no life for you. It makes me feel guilty. I'm unhappy every minute. I never know whether I'm going to freak out, whether my head is going to get worse. I'm going to try. I'm going to every minute of therapy I can, as much hypnosis as she'll do. I'm going to force myself to be a normal lesbian. But if that doesn't start showing some results by December 1st, I'm going to cut off the phone calls and have the temporary separation Shirl suggested."

"Andy, no! How can you judge whether anything will work in the long run on the basis of just three weeks? That's no time at all."

"For the state I'm in, it's plenty of time. Just three weeks of my head exploding!"

"But maybe you should have less pressure instead of more. Maybe the pressure of the deadline won't help."

"Maybe it won't, but I've got to do it this way. I can't go slow—that isn't my way."

Another time Andy called and said, "I do have some good news, honey."

"Good news? *You* have *good* news? I can hardly believe it."

"Ouch. Tough, aren't you? Yes, punkin, my doctor says the clot is clearing up."

"Andy! Honey, that's so wonderful. I knew it would. I was sure."

"They can't kill off the kid. Ain't no way."

One Saturday night Andy called and said, "I'm at a bar, Bad. What do you think of that? I'm at a bar and someone is trying to pick me up."

"What kind of bar? Straight or gay?" The music was so loud that she could hardly hear Andy.

"It's a gay bar—a tough one. Thought I should mingle with my own kind. You should see some of the women here. You wouldn't like them at all."

"Eileen types, I suppose?"

"Some of them make Eileen look like a china doll. Are they tough. The woman I've been drinking with looks pretty mean. It might be hard to say 'no' to her."

"I thought you didn't like bars much and weren't too crazy about hanging around with tough people."

"I don't like it. I just felt like I should come here."

"That's clever. To convince yourself that lesbianism is something unappealing? It doesn't make any sense to go to the kind of place you never liked before."

"I don't know. Maybe I'm changing. Maybe if I'm a lesbian I'll be cold—or promiscuous."

"Thanks a lot, dearest."

"I still care enough about you to come to the phone booth and call you. But I am getting colder. Maybe I've been through too much. Maybe it's better for me to be around this type—maybe that's what I really am. If I were like you, I'd be with you, wouldn't I?"

"I don't know." She pictured some impossibly dark and seedy bar—probably the place where Andy was looked a little better than that—populated by women who were female versions of Hell's Angels. How silly—she had never seen anything like that herself. Some older women were large and wore butch clothes, but they seemed lonely, not particularly sinister.

"Maybe I am cold. Maybe I'd better go get a drink to warm me up. I've had plenty, but I don't care."

"Drinking? Is it drinking now? Good grief, what next—never mind, I won't want to know. How is it that you can be with those women and not me?"

"I don't *want* them, so it's easier to be around them."

"Oh, that's just craziness. Why don't you get out of that damn bar and go home?"

"Oh, my, she's getting tough."

"Well, I suppose I'd better, if you're going to hang around with tough types."

"Maybe I'll let my friends out there buy me another drink. I don't have much money."

"That's clever."

"Never said I was smart, did I? But I do know how to play tricks on this type. I've been going to the bars the last couple of days, after work. I get them to buy me a few drinks, then split before they know what's hit them."

"An admirable practice. What's the point of leading them on?"

"Why not? I have nothing better to do with my time. Maybe I'm getting mean."

"Maybe you are."

"Ouch, you weren't supposed to say that."

"Sorry."

"No, you aren't. Okay, maybe I'll be good. Maybe I'll go home. You know I need you. Why else would I call?"

"To make me as miserable as you are?"

"Great! See what I'm doing? Maybe I shouldn't call you at all."

Maybe, Brenda thought, the hidden thing Shirl found inside you is that you like to torture me. Aloud she said, "Please don't say that. You know I want you to call."

"You love me even when I'm dumb enough to call you from this bar?"

"Yes."

"I do love you, too. Maybe I will go home after all."

Brenda was breaking down more and more visibly. The dark circles under her eyes that had first become apparent in September had now become permanent features, carving an ever deeper groove. She drank more Cokes now, dashing to the machine downstairs in the paper's office building the moment she emptied one. Her conversation about subjects other than Andy dwindled. She said little in meetings. Although the chief features of every day were phone calls with Andy, she still enjoyed opening the newspaper's mail and processing it all immediately, entering the subscriptions in the ledger with compulsive dedication, as proof of her continued functioning in the world. She told herself that she was the best office worker the newspaper ever had because no one else had ever processed the mail so quickly. She came to the office five days a week, while Dolly, mindful that the office job was supposed to be three-fifths time, came three or four days. Brenda felt that her life would crack if she missed a day.

Andy kept calling.

"I wish I was depressed—or sad. I don't even know if I can be sad any more. My grandmother's cat got run over by a car this morning and I don't feel anything. I used to really care about that cat. I'm getting so cold that it scares me."

Brenda agreed more than she wanted to admit. Not caring about the death of one's cat seemed to her the last reaches of moral estrangement from one's true nature. "Oh, the poor cat. Poor you. You've just been through too much."

"Maybe too much to care about anybody else." (Of course, Brenda thought. If she doesn't care about her cat, how can she care about me? She saw herself stretched out on the highway, with Andy proclaiming, in the same tone, that she just couldn't care.) "I used to worry so much about the people who came into my office. Women beaten by their husbands. I was so angry—I'd do anything to help them. I don't feel that way now. I just do the routine—don't ask them all of the questions I should. Don't talk to them as long as I should. I think so much about the shocks and the hypnosis and my sexuality that I can't think of anything else. Maybe I'll go to a straight bar and pick up some man to pay my doctor bills. What does it matter anymore?"

"Don't say those things. Somewhere inside you must know that it still matters." Brenda tried not to show her reaction to the comment about men.

"Must I?"

"Yes, you must. It hasn't been that long."

"It may not be long, but I may be a different person."

15

"I'll talk to you later," Andy said. "I've got to see my lawyer. Some radical lawyers from another group are working on a little something for me." There was a hint of mystery in Andy's voice — and Brenda had long since learned that the mysteries Andy hinted at were always real.

"A little what? A little tort, or a little murder trial? I'd expect the latter more than the former. What's happening?"

"Nothing much. Nothing to bother you with," she said, clearly conveying the opposite.

For days she teased Andy to find out what the lawyer was for. Andy's references to the lawyer became more frequent, and she would add that she had "to do work for her lawyer."

"Whatever the matter is, I'll stand by you," Brenda finally urged. "Only please tell me—or write, if it can't be told over the phone." Ever security-conscious because of the radical newspaper, she thought about taps—amd asked this kind of question over her own phone, which was somewhat less likely than the newspaper phone to be bugged (if her phone was bugged, by the way, what sex-filled moments the agent must have heard). "Are there charges against you? Are you possibly going to be on trial?"

"On trial? Me? What for?" Andy sounded more than annoyed. "What do you think I am? What could I have done?"

"Who knows? Everything is so horrible and melodramatic. I wondered if you could have attacked that man who shocked you —

you've mentioned the possibility. And he'd richly deserve it."

Andy was somewhat mollified. "He'll get his, but not like that. It's all going to be legal. There's going to be a suit. There are three other black women that he did the same things to, and we're all in the suit together."

"God, three more women. Did he have to torture every black lesbian he could find?"

"He tried. I've heard them tell parts of their stories—it's pretty grim."

"What shape are they in? Are they still lesbians?" She was a little ashamed of the obvious self-interest prompting this question.

"One of them is doing fine, the others not so well. She was just in there for a few days. One of them was in even longer than me, six weeks."

"God, how horrible. And horrible for you to hear it, too."

"I don't know. Sometimes I feel really close to them and sympathetic, other times I just feel like I've been through it so many times . . . I get cold about that too. We're trying to prepare our testimony. That's the 'work for my lawyers' I told you about. I have to try to remember every detail, what happened on each day. That's hard. I keep blocking. Everything runs together."

"That does sound hard. You have to keep going over it all both for this and the therapy."

"Yes, it's hard. I'm trying to use the hypnosis to remember things for the trial. That isn't much fun. And writing it all down so the lawyers can use it—I'm no writer. I wish I were."

"You could have a writer by your side in a minute to write down the details as you mention them." She let herself joke.

"Never give up, do you? No, silly, you can't be with me. I wouldn't want you to hear all this. Ugh." She let her voice shudder.

"I'd love to be there by your side. You're so brave. It's wonderful that there's a way of standing up to him. Civil suit or criminal suit?"

"Maybe both. Civil for now. They're trying to get money from him—maybe the D.A.'ll do something, too, but I don't think so. If they get money, I won't take any. I just want everybody to know him for what he is."

"You *are* the greatest. Although not taking the money seems a little too noble—the least he could do is pay your shrink bills. It's costing you plenty to try to undo what he did."

"No. I won't take any money."

It was Thanksgiving morning and Brenda minded very much that

Andy was not there. Not that they had anything much to be thankful for or anyone to be thankful to, but it was a day when you couldn't help being aware that most people supposedly were with loved ones having an occasion. Never mind that Brenda had actually hated most of those occasions — except for the food itself — she wanted occasions anyway.

Since she had married Ted, she had made pumpkin pies (from scratch) every year. Ted cooked the pumpkins and mashed the pulp; Brenda mixed and cooked the pie. She believed in her pumpkin pies. She didn't bake a pie this year because she now associated her domesticity with Andy and wanted to bake pies only for Andy.

But she would have a turkey—she couldn't give up everything until she had pie in the sky with Andy. Turkey was simply too fundamental to give up.

There might not be love at the table, but there was familiarity, and that was what most people sought on Thanksgiving.

At least Ted probably would not hurt her in any new ways.

He had baked acorn squash in butter, spices, and brown sugar and made a mixture of sweet potato, orange, and brown sugar. How hard to give up cooking like this, even to be a lesbian.

"This is fantastic! You're a wonderful cook. I've never figured out how anyone could do that much with vegetables." She wanted to be appreciative.

He beamed with pride: his cooking was one of the great joys of his heart. If only he were gay—how much easier the separation would be.

"Thank you. I wanted to try something new with the sweet potatoes, but I figured you wouldn't like it. Those squash were tough to cut; it took a long time to cook them."

"You've really gone to a lot of work. Thank you. Nothing tastes better than Thanksgiving food."

She was glad that she was with Ted because she could peel the turkey and eat almost all of the skin while it was still warm. Mouse could stand on the table, as usual, gulping down turkey so fast that he almost choked. The cat was served first, as always.

They both ate happily, great lovers of food if not of each other, though occasionally their eyes twinkled a little at each other's peculiarities. She could almost feel sentimental about having a nice ex-husband.

"While I was sitting here today," he said, "I was trying to make calculations. How shall we split up the furniture—and everything. What about the cookbooks?" This was not a departure from cheerfulness.

"Oh, no, you've weakened me by giving me good food before the discussion. Despite that, I think the fact that you earn $20,000 a year and I earn, at the moment, $200 a month—though I hope to earn more soon—should be significant. You can afford to buy things; I can't." She put some stuffing in her mouth.

"That's true—my take-home pay doesn't come to that much, though."

"The bedroom set is yours, of course."

"Of course." Her mother had given it to her when she was nine.

"But I'd like the other sofa bed."

"Yes, but I'll want it back when you can buy something. Mouse likes it so much—and it's the only piece of furniture that he's allowed to scratch."

"That's fine." He scratched the cat behind its ears.

"The cat's mine. That's the main thing." She blazed slightly, ready to strike if challenged.

"Of course. You're his mother. He's your cat." He ate a mouthful of squash.

It was true, Mouse was her cat, but her most paranoid fantasies involved Ted hurting and kidnapping Mouse.

"I want the dining room set, too. I bought it. I love it. I know I bought it for us, but I want it. I'll never be able to buy anything this good again." She was defensive because they had selected the long, massive Spanish table together, though she had picked it out first and then brought him to see it. He loved it too and polished it religiously, with two coats of wax, which she did not.

"You can have the table," he grunted, without a show of regret.

She was impressed. Guiltily, she asked, "Could I have the sofa and chairs, too? I know your parents gave them to us, but you can afford others and I can't. And they go with the dining room furniture."

He paused. "Yes. You can have the wall hangings, too," he said.

She was pleased but a little amazed. She had bought all of their half-dozen Latin American hangings, except for the serape that her parents had bought on their honeymoon, but she had expected more of a struggle. "Thank you."

"I just want the painting we bought on our honeymoon."

He had been so proud of it—their only "original" painting, it had cost a whole seventy-five dollars. He believed that the artist who had painted the nice New England winter scene would become famous—the snowflakes were so delicate.

She had liked the painting; they had hunted through little seacoast craft store after craft store to find it. But by the time they had returned home, she had tired of both the painting and the marriage, though she would not tell him.

"Of course—and the lithographs, too." She didn't want them either.

"And the pressure cooker—I can't cook without it. And the deep fryer."

"Of course. You know I never use either of them anyway. But could I keep the blender? You use it more than I do, but you can more easily get another."

"All right." He began scooping second helpings onto his plate.

"And can I keep the dishes? My mother gave them to us." They had a fifty-dollar set of sturdy green and brown Franciscan china, Madeira pattern.

"Yes, but I want one set of the pots and pans."

They had two complete teflon sets, given them by his relatives.

"Of course. And you can choose." She finished her squash.

"The black one."

She winced very slightly; she preferred that one, too. Well, she must be civilized; he was giving up quite a lot.

"Can I keep my mother's silverplate?"

"I never liked that anyway. I want the *good* stainless steel."

"Yuch." She would admit to being a snob about the weight of silverware in her hands. Eating with stainless steel had never felt natural. Born with a silver spoon in her mouth. Well, yes, she was.

She sliced herself some more turkey.

"And you can't have all the cookbooks," he said between mouthfuls.

"No, of course not, though I want most of them. Let's each pick the cookbooks that we use the most recipes from and xerox or copy out the recipes the other one wants. Okay?"

"That's fine."

She was finishing her second helping of turkey. He had already finished his second helpings. "This was a nice Thanksgiving dinner."

"Yes." He was already clearing off the plates: he didn't like to stay at the table because his mother had been rooted to her dining room table, and hadn't let him leave for an hour after the meal.

Brenda had never been pleased with his haste to end dinner, but now it was fine. They had run out of things to say.

The first thing in the morning—that is, after rising, feeding and petting Mouse, dressing, reading the newspaper, and exchanging a brief greeting on the phone with Andy, Brenda was off to buy her love a ring for Christmas. Andy had hinted that she, too, was giving a ring.

No doubt rings were a part of a horrible patriarchal history, a symbol of bondage. No doubt they were as anachronistic as the corset. However, she would give her love a ring, and that was that. She wanted Andy to see the ring every hour and remember her. Of course she believed that she would be remembered without the ring; the ring was more than a reminder, it was a display. Display mattered, formalities mattered, even in a radical world. There could be no human world without symbols.

She entered a small Connecticut Avenue jewelry store that specialized in antiques. An old-fashioned ring for an old-fashioned love. Brenda didn't care for contemporary settings. She wished she knew more about Andy's taste, but hoped it was the same. She had intended to buy a ring with tiny stones, with some color in them, preferably in an intricate Victorian design. Amethysts would be best because their color was closest to lavender.

She studied the trays of rings over and over, not seeing precisely what she wanted. She wondered whether the clerks thought the woman in jeans and jean jacket too grubby to be shopping for their rings.

There was a delicate cluster of small garnets, but it cost over one hundred dollars. She had told herself that fifty was her limit—after all, it was far more than she could afford. But she couldn't afford anything, so what did that matter? She was determined to deviate only a little from her limit. Andy would be embarrassed if she got something too obviously expensive.

There weren't any amethysts. Lapis lazuli was also beautiful.

"May I help you?" asked a middle-aged woman clerk, with bouffant hair and glasses on a string, who was not enchanted with Brenda's slow and deliberate buying methods.

"Not yet, thank you." She would not be rushed.

Finally, she asked to see two lapis lazuli, one garnet, and one opal. The saleswoman brought them out. Brenda stared at them, slipping on her fingers those that would fit. Of course Andy's fingers were slimmer.

She wished she could give all of them, she wished she could keep all of them for herself. Brenda had a love not so much for jewelry as for jewels.

After many minutes of contemplation, she picked a lapis lazuli ring that had a small dark blue center surrounded by five golden, lattice-work petals with a small blue stone on each. It is beautiful, she decided. It is not beautiful enough, but nothing could be beautiful enough. I hope she likes lapis—she wears a lot of blue.

The little ring cost seventy dollars. She paid for it, and left it to be fitted to Andy's ring size.

Andy called and life began again. Brenda leaned and rubbed the cat under the chin. "How are you, Andy Dandy?"

"Okay. Shirl has been doing something I'm not too crazy about." Much of the warmth went out of her voice.

"What?" Visions of tortures designed to drag buried secrets from Andy's brain filled her mind.

"Oh, she's been trying to get me to drop out of the trial, or not to testify in person, anyway. She says it's too much for me, too soon. She couldn't talk me out of it. So she talked to my lawyers. I don't want her doing that."

Brenda's voice was suddenly strained. "What do you mean? Does she think that digging up inside you would hurt you? Aren't you doing that anyway?"

"Yeah, but I guess she thinks I could fall apart if I went on the stand and had to go through it all in public and face the cross-examination. Maybe I could flip out completely."

I never thought of that. How selfish I am. All I thought of was her testifying bravely, me sitting admiringly, supportively watching her, and everybody at the paper finally believing her and respecting her. Good for me—not seeing that it might break her down, make her worse.

"Oh, baby, how awful. I hadn't thought of that. It's true that questioning of a woman who's accusing a man of mistreating her can be brutal. Maybe you aren't up to it yet."

"The trial won't be for months. They aren't even ready to file yet."

"But Shirley knows that, doesn't she? And she still thinks you shouldn't do it?" Everything in their lives was staked on the premise that Shirl was right. She must assume that Shirl was right now. At last she had a chance to help Shirl, to help the treatment.

"I guess so. That's what she keeps telling me."

"Couldn't you give testimony some other way—by deposition or whatever?"

"Yes, but I don't want to. I've got to face him. He'll be there! I don't know what I'll do if I see him sitting there. That frightens me. Maybe I will break down. But it's worth it. What does it matter, anyway. Going crazy couldn't be any worse than the way things are now."

"Yes, it could. You could be back in the power of people like him."

"Oh, I guess Shirl would find a better place to lock me up in."

"Don't say such a thing. Aren't there other women who will testify anyway, women who apparently won't be affected as badly?"

"Yeah, there are. But I should do my bit, too."

"Good grief, you sound like a soldier enlisting. 'Other people are going to face the bullets, so I should too.' What good has that kind of heroism done for the world? Doesn't assuming that kind of risk mean putting too low a value on everybody's life, not just your own?"

Andy's voice sounded angry. "Don't call me a soldier. I just want to stop him. I don't want him to do to anyone else what he did to me."

The angry voice frightened Brenda, but she continued. "Of course you want to stop him, and you're going to. Of course you're going to help the trial. But maybe you could do that without doing anything that Shirley warns you against. If they already have somebody going on the stand, maybe your deposition would do just as much as your going on the stand would."

"Maybe it would. I don't know. I don't care. What happens to me doesn't matter."

"Of course it matters! Risking your mind is much more dreadful than risking your body. You don't have to risk your sanity for anyone."

"Maybe we shouldn't keep on talking about this. I've been angry at Shirl and now I'm getting angry at you." The voice was not only angry, it was cold.

The tone did frighten Brenda, but she felt that she shouldn't let that stop her. She only had a short time until Andy cut off their phone connection, and she must use that time to save her once again, to persuade Andy not to take another rash course. She would try to save Andy, even if in doing so she lost her, Brenda resolved.

"Maybe we should keep on talking anyway. I'm worried. I don't suppose Shirl would have said those things unless she knew what she was talking about. She does seem to care about you. Maybe you should go along with her."

"You and she agree. You just want to keep me alive and going no matter what."

"Well, that's important."

"Maybe it is; maybe it isn't. To me, it isn't. I want to get him."

"You're going along with Shirl about me, but not about this. I don't feel too great about that. Maybe you hate him more than you love me."

"I don't know which is stronger. I don't think about it that way."

But I do, Bad thought.

The phone calls ended on December 1st, and Bad knew that she was alone, that Andy would not be calling tomorrow. She did not face the future with the brash confidence of a Scarlett O'Hara. It seemed all too likely that she might never see Andy again.

No, she wouldn't believe that. The connection between them was so powerful that it would surely survive anything. Surely the dependence would bring Andy back. Dependence was better than nothing. And if they both felt dependent, surely that meant that they were interdependent, which sounded so much healthier.

She would wait. She would write letters. She would try to be calm.

It is only a question of waiting, she told herself after the first few days. Anyone can wait—it takes no special skill. All I have to do is read to pass the time. All I need is persistence—well, I have plenty of that.

16

One evening Ted announced, "I'm going out with a woman tonight. I have to hurry and change my clothes."

It had been almost two years since the last time that Brenda had made love with him, about a year and a half since she had told him that she was a lesbian and would leave him eventually. At last, she thought.

"Good." She paused. "What's her name?"

"Laura." He was busily pulling shirts out of the closet and stripping off his own.

"Do you mind if I ask a few questions?"

"No." He selected a beige shirt with thin pale blue stripes. "Do you think this would look good with the blue sweater?"

"Yes, very good. What does she do?"

"She's a biologist. Works at HEW." He buttoned the shirt with heightening speed.

"Did you meet her at work?"

"Yes. She isn't in my office. We met at a seminar." Ted pulled the sweater on over his head.

"I'm glad."

"So am I. I have to get going." He messed around with his wallet, then hurried off.

Brenda went to the kitchen and began mixing some hamburger with worcestershire and soy sauce for her dinner. She was slightly surprised, but perfectly calm: she felt very little—but she certainly didn't feel numb.

She woke up at three a.m. to go to the bathroom. While passing the double bed, she glanced to see if Ted was there. No. Just a flicker of worry crossed her mind. I hope he's in bed with Laura and not out in a wreck somewhere. No, that was too silly. Of course he was with Laura. She was pleased and perhaps a little surprised to see how absolutely little she cared. She wouldn't have been startled to discover that a person in her situation might feel a twinge of unwarranted jealousy, but it wasn't there. Brenda went back to sleep.

Brenda decided to make Christmas cookies for Andy. It took her several shopping trips to find a fruitcake tin to mail them in.

Christmas cookies were a major tradition for her. Some of her earliest memories were of cutting out Christmas trees and gingerbread men. At first, her mother had made the batter and rolled the dough, then Brenda cut the cookies and decorated them with sparkles. Soon, she was doing the whole process herself. She still baked sugar cookies every year; they reminded her that life was not relentlessly sophisticated. Some of the old simplicity was still possible. A cookie was a cookie.

She had all of the old animal cookie cutters: her mother had mailed them to her when she married. A squirrel, a rabbit, a dog (a Scottie), a horse, and a butterfly lived in the cookie cutter box with a star, a Christmas tree, a fingernail moon, a heart, and a santa claus. A few years ago she had found a camel, a cat, an elephant, and a giraffe.

This year the cookies would be for Andy, a symbol of the domestic life she hoped to have with Andy, with electric shocks only a distant memory. The cookies would be an attempt to show Andy that she was still calm, an attempt to transmit that calm to Andy. If you treat problems calmly, perhaps they may dissolve. If you meet a tiger, offer it catnip.

Solemnly, she decorated each cookie, deciding whether it should be green, red, or multi-colored. She made many red hearts.

The cookie baking consumed a day—the happiest day that she had had in a while. Brenda ate the broken cookies and packed all of the others in the tin. None could go to Ted, because they were a present for Andy. Contented, she wrapped and mailed the tin.

She was not so quick to clean up after making the cookies. Neither she nor Ted had washed a dish since Thanksgiving. "Why don't you wash the dishes?" he had said.

"Why don't you? Most of them are yours. You use so many pans. You can't cook the simplest dish without using three pans."

"I've always done more housework than you have, and I'm tired of it. I'm not going to do a single thing more than you do."

"It's true that you've done more housework," she admitted. "I'm not denying that. But you agreed to, because of school and my meetings. And you also make more of a mess. Why don't we each just clean up our share?"

"Will you clean up the kitchen now?"

"No—just part of it."

"Forget it—you'll never do your share."

"I think you're wrong. As long as we're talking, there's something else I'd like to ask you."

"What?" he asked suspiciously.

"Could you *please* stop walking about the house naked and half-naked. It bothers me very much. It really turns me off. Surely now that you're involved with someone else, too, you can see that we need to have privacy about our bodies. And please *stop* walking into the bathroom when I'm on the toilet."

Ted's face reddened and his eyes glared. "I'm sorry you've decided you don't like my body anymore, but that's just too bad. I'm not going to worry about dressing in my own home. You'll just have to get used to it."

"Ted, please. My lover was electric shocked to try to make her sleep with men. Sometimes I fear that she may wind up with a man out of desperation. That's what I think of when I see your body now. I don't want to see a man's body. I'm sorry—I didn't want to insult you. I've tried to be quiet about this for a long time, but I can't anymore. Please understand that I'm going through something extreme and be considerate."

"You're going through something extreme, all right. No, I won't be forced to dress in my own home."

"You dressed in your parents' home. You didn't run around naked or with just that falling-open bathrobe there."

"This is different. This is my home, and I have a right to be comfortable. You've done everything you can to make me feel uncomfortable in my own home."

"Please, Ted—I'll do more housework if you'll only do that."

"No way. I don't want to talk about it anymore." He glowered, radiating anger.

So the apartment became filthier and filthier. Neither of them was willing to do anything. They no longer ate together. Each ate alone, with a book, even if the other was in the room. Each washed whatever dish and pan was necessary to prepare food for her or himself, no more. Brenda changed the cat litter.

The dirt and untidyness harmonized with the state of despair that was Brenda's true state of mind beneath the pretense of hope. If she couldn't have Andy, what did it matter if her kitchen smelled and some of the plates had a several-week-old crust of food on them? If you slept alone, who cared how many months the sheets went without washing? Why bother to make anything pleasant for Ted?

When this naked man would dart into the bathroom to run his tub while she was on the toilet, he seemed increasingly like a rapist. She felt unable to get away, to avert her eyes quickly enough. She couldn't go anywhere in her apartment without having naked male flesh thrust in front of her eyes.

She tried to be rational, to remind herself that initially she had found him attractive, that he had, after all, been very nice to her. She ought to be more tolerant—at least while she was living on his money, for the next (she hoped, few) months. She was broke—she had less than two hundred dollars left and owed the collective more than a month's more work to pay for her phone bills. The November bill had been worse than all the others, astronomical enough almost to wipe her out completely—more than four hundred dollars.

Still, she could not forgive Ted for forcing his nakedness on her, now that he knew how it upset her. He was asserting some sexual control over her still, against her will, and that was intolerable. If he had been the sensitive man she had thought, surely he wouldn't want anyone who found him physically repulsive to see him. Her anger grew.

Brenda dreaded Christmas. If she had had the money, she might have fled to her mother's in Los Angeles, but that was not possible. Dolly was going to visit friends. Brenda felt deserted, isolated.

Every day she waited anxiously for her gift from Andy or for some word, some gesture. A few days before Christmas a package arrived.

She extracted an incredibly ordinary-looking Christmas card, with red holly on it, the kind of card insurance salesmen send customers. It said, "Merry Christmas to Bad from Andy."

Brenda bit her lip. Not a single endearment. Things couldn't be good. Andy must have been angry at her last letter.

She fished through the layers of tissue, the cat's paw following her, and extracted a small box wrapped in red paper.

At least she gave me a ring. She must love me if she gave me a ring.

She tore the paper off the box. The cat, more ambitious than usual, positively grabbed at the little box. She gave him the paper.

Her first feeling was incredible disappointment. Oh damn, I don't like her taste, I don't like it at all. Why can't she have taste like mine, or know what mine is?

The ring looked to her like a class ring. It was gold, and bore her initials in capital letters, "BAD."

She put it on the third finger of her left hand. She had never worn any rings there but her wedding ring. She had stopped wearing that three-and-a-half years before.

The ring seemed solipsistic. It had *her own name* on it, BAD, as if to say she was married to herself. Yes, she had herself, yes, she knew she was alone. This just rubbed it in. Could it at least have said "Bad +Andy." She burst into tears.

It was the wrong ring. The wrong card. Not a single affectionate word, not a single unnecessary word. She was alone—everything else was just pretense. She didn't even dare to call Andy and thank her. What kind of exchange of rings was it if you didn't dare to say thank you?

How dare I be so cold as to care about the appearance of the ring, she scolded herself, and felt ashamed, but she knew that the appearance wasn't the real problem.

She scrutinized the ring, determined to find something attractive about it. Sure enough, if you looked at it in the light, the flat surface on which the initials were engraved shone. It was golden—Andy was golden. That was how she would rationalize it.

That night, she felt less alone. She lay in bed twisting the ring. She kissed its surface. When she woke in the middle of the night, she could feel it there. Whenever she felt low, she kissed the ring—if there was no one around.

On Christmas morning there was no call from Andy.

She gave Ted her presents, nicely wrapped, and he gave her a large paper bag. Ted never wrapped anything, much as she had pleaded and scolded him to in the days when she cared. She loved unwrapping pretty packages—it reminded her of her childhood, and she didn't care how bourgeois or commercial it was. Gifts comforted her.

Brenda reached in the bag and pulled out a large red plaid wool jacket. It was exactly the same as the one he was giving his girl-friend.

"You liked Laura's, so I thought you'd like one too."

She could hardly suppress the laughter. "The same thing? The exact same thing! I'll bet you aren't telling Laura that."

"No."

"That's hysterical." She laughed.

He was a bit defensive. "It's a good jacket."

When he went off to see Laura, Brenda was still giggling.

A few minutes before midnight, the telephone rang. She dived for it.

"Hello!"

"Hi there, Bad. Merry Christmas. I just thought I'd say hello."

"I knew you would. Thank you. The ring is wonderful—I love it. I kiss it and touch it when I wake up at night. Did you get the thank-you letter?"

"Yes. Uh—did you ever get the letter I sent?"

"No, what letter?"

"That's weird. I sent one."

"Maybe you didn't put on a stamp? Well, the post office is so bad. We've never lost a letter before. Maybe I wasn't meant to get it."

"That's really weird. Maybe I'll write and tell you what it said. Did you have a good Christmas?"

"Sort of. Though I missed you. How are the hallucinations? The nightmares?"

"Both better."

"Better—that's wonderful—fantastic. It will work out, really it will."

"I don't know."

17

On Monday after Christmas, two letters came, both with Andy's return post-box address. One seemed to have photos in it, so she opened that first.

There was just a sheet of stationery saying, "Some more pictures of Andy for you." Three pictures of Andy posing in a living room decorated for Christmas tensed her every muscle. Andy was thinner, well groomed, and smiling broadly. Her face lacked the softness of previous pictures. The expression seemed sardonic, with pretended raucous glee, almost a sneer. I wouldn't trust the woman in that picture, Brenda said to herself. That's not Andy.

She opened the other envelope.

Dear Bad,

I don't know how that other letter got lost, but I'm trying to remember what it said and copy it.

I've been trying to do something good, to try to keep other women from going through what I've gone through. I can't stand to think of any more women being shocked. That does matter more to me than anything. More than you.

I don't love you anymore. I stopped loving you the night after Thanksgiving when you tried to talk me out of the trial. You don't understand what it means to me. Shirl told me later that she was just trying to test me to see if I was really determined to do it. I am. She's going to help me.

I have talked all this over with Shirl and know what I want. Don't tell me I'm confused.

You and I don't have anything in common. I care about helping people. When Maxy and I were together, we used to help other people. You don't care about anybody but the two of us. That's not how I want to live.

131

You write about feminism and helping people, but it's all just words for you. I'm tired of your words.

What is the women's movement all about, anyway? Your newspaper friends don't seem to care much about other women, seeing how they acted about me and how they treated you. I don't want to know people like that. Why should I want to be a lesbian if that's what they're like?

I'm tired of worrying about how you're going to feel about things. I'm the one who was shocked, not you. You can talk about it, but you don't know how it feels. I'm the one who has to live with it.

I don't ever want to see you again. I don't want to talk to you on the phone. I won't read any more letters. I'm grateful to you for helping me when I was suicidal, but it's over. We don't have anything to say to each other. I'm tired of worrying about you.

Don't try to get in touch. Just drop it. I don't feel anything for you.

Andy

Brenda crumpled the letter. She paced up and down the apartment, shaking. "No! No! No! No! No!" She screamed and moaned, feeling as if she never wanted to stop but would remain suspended throughout eternity pacing and screaming, "no." It didn't matter if she went crazy—if she screamed long enough, she would go crazy. Good.

The ring. I won't take it off. Ever.

No, it doesn't mean anything if she doesn't love me.

I just got it. I don't want to give it up. Goddamn, she gives me a ring, I wear it for a week, show it to all my friends. Then she makes a fool of me again. I'm tired of looking like a fool.

The ring looked all too beautiful and desirable now.

At nine the next morning, she called Andy at work.

"Hello?"

"Hello. It's me. I got your letter. I guess you don't want to talk?"

"There isn't any point."

"I want to send one letter. Just one. Please. To defend myself. Please read it. Just one letter?"

"All right."

Crying, Brenda hurried to her pen and paper. Why should I have to feel like some kind of criminal, she thought. As if I had treated Andy horribly instead of trying to support her through everything. No doubt I'm patronizing and all, but oh goddamn this is too much.

Her hand shook as she wrote,

My beloved Andy,

I cannot stop loving though you have stopped loving me. I'll love you always and I am deeply grateful to have known you and had your love.

I do think the way you lashed out at me was unfair. Of course I have plenty of faults, of course I'm too obsessed with you, but how you could accuse me of not caring about helping people I don't know. I don't do as much as I should—nobody does. But, goddamnit, when I answered your letter to the paper and talked to you about suicide I didn't know that you were going to be my lover. I didn't know that you were pretty. I didn't know that you were someone I would enjoy being with. You were just a woman somewhere who might kill herself and I would have done the same for anyone.

Of course "helping" people is an ego trip, I know that, but that's true for you as well as for me. That's true for anybody. And it isn't one of the worst ego trips people can get into, either.

I tried to talk you out of the trial because Shirl said so. How was I supposed to know that she was just testing you? Why assume that she was acting in good faith and I wasn't? Remember that I also went along when she said things that had an adverse impact on us. Remember that I urged you to go back to her even though I knew she thought we should have a "temporary separation." "Temporary," hell.

Of course I care whether other women get shocked. What kind of monster do you think I am? You said there were other women who would testify and who wouldn't be hurt by it.

I was really proud of you for wanting to testify in the first place— don't you remember? I was secretly so proud and felt that I'd be vindicated in front of all my newspaper friends who doubted you. A trial was real news that they couldn't deny. I tried to hide how strongly I felt that. I didn't try to stop you until Shirl was opposed to it. Don't you remember?

You say that everything is "just words" for me. Does that mean that a writer can never be a good person? Can't words ever help or console? I thought there were times when my words did help—you said that you kept reciting "live, damn you, live," when you were in the hospital. Isn't that some kind of help? My love for you is not just a word, it's never been just a word. I've always been ready to do anything for you. Why should you assume that my feminism is any more superficial than that? I use words, many words, but I don't use them without meaning something. I don't tell a person "I love you" without meaning that I'll stand by her no matter what. My words are an attempt to express real feelings, to explore real problems.

You make me feel so terrible about my writing that I don't feel I can write. I'm not a phony, but if writers are by definition, what am I?

I'm sorry that I failed you. I didn't mean to fail you. I would have given anything not to have failed you.

I hope that things go well for you. I am proud of your commitment and do hope the trial goes well. Much love always,

Bad

This attack on her writing made Brenda feel that Andy wanted not only to leave her but to leave her with nothing.

Maybe I won't write. How can I write about feminism if the woman I have loved has challenged my feminism and found it wanting? What kind of feminist am I if I couldn't help the woman I love?

For the first time in Brenda's life, the thought of writing was not a consolation. Since she was sixteen, she had consoled herself in every painful situation by promising herself that she would write about it, that her pain would be useful because it would be expressed and the situation would be transcended. She had seen writing as the main purpose of her life.

Every day was another step in a long road of days leading away from the time when she had been Andy's lover. She was quite sure that the best part of her life was over.

It annoyed her to see that Ted's apparently unambitious and practical romance was succeeding while hers with Andy had failed. Once, hoping to get him out of the house more often, she had asked why he didn't spend more than two nights a week with Laura.

"Two nights is enough," he said.

Two nights is enough! The complacency behind that remark disgusted her. She would not want to be part of a relationship in which two nights were, automatically, enough. Two nights might be a necessary accommodation to circumstances, but "enough" was appalling.

Of course she had known that he would find somebody. Eligible men always did find women willing to accommodate them or give their lives to them. Even men like Strom Thurmond, Southern racist, could get a woman. But she could walk through hell for her Eurydice and still be left alone. She smouldered with resentment. She was not jealous of his body—no, quite the opposite. Jealous of the fact that though he was no more intelligent, better educated, creative, serious, tender, passionate, or better-looking than she (and of course she believed that she surpassed him in some of those traits), he would be the one who would easily obtain a woman's love, or what passed for it.

The December phone bill came. Though it was moderate compared to earlier bills, being slightly less than two hundred dollars (because late November had been included in it), she did not have the money to pay for it. Previous phone bills had exhausted her funds, and Christmas had finished them off. She had, however, paid off her time at the newspaper and would go back to receiving her fifty-dollar-a-week salary in January. Her term as office worker ended in February; she would have saved nothing.

One evening she mentioned the phone bill to Ted. She had already told him about the end of her relationship with Andy, and he had responded with a few words of cool sympathy.

"The December phone bill arrived today. It's less than the last few have been, but I'm afraid I don't have the money to pay for it. It's a bit high because it includes Thanksgiving, when Andy and I were still speaking. It's $168; I have only $42 in the bank."

Ted, who had been puttering with a special knapsack that he was making for himself, wheeled around to face her and glared. "This has got to be the end of it! You've gone crazy! Spending all that money on that bitch who won't even come to Washington to see you. I'll pay this bill if you promise not to blow any more money on phone calls with her."

Every muscle in her longed to lunge at him and attack, though he was in so much better physical shape that the idea was ridiculous. She hated him at that moment for having more money than she did and supporting her.

She yelled also. "Don't you dare talk about the woman I love that way. You've never had the troubles she has. I won't ever promise not to speak to her. You know damn well that she cut me off and won't speak to me. I'd give anything to be able to speak to her again."

She saw him as the patriarch demanding control of his household. "This can't happen again. I won't let it happen again. I'll do what I damn please. I'm just asking you to pay this one phone bill. If there are others, I certainly won't ask you for help. You have no right to impose conditions on me, and I won't ever recognize that right."

"I have a right to see that we don't go broke because of your girl-friends."

"Don't say 'we.' I'm the one who's broke. I've spent my own money on phone calls, not yours. And I'm damned sorry that I've lived on yours. Don't worry—I won't much longer. I can't wait to get away from you. You don't own me, though I guess you like the feeling that you do."

He saw that he had misfired: he didn't want her to leave. He tried to sound reasonable though he was still angry. "I've never minded supporting you. I've always said I'd help you out until you got the Ph.D. I've never complained. I've never tried to control you. I'm worried about you. You can't keep on like this. Why can't you find somebody who isn't crazy—somebody normal, like I did?"

"To sleep with for a normal, functional two nights a week? No thank you. Love isn't always practical. It may disrupt your life. But at least it should be real, not based on convenience. I'd rather be alone—obviously, I will be alone."

"That's up to you."

"It certainly is. Stop worrying about your damn money. I won't be around to spend it much longer. I appreciate your helping me in school, but I'm not going to grovel about it. I'd do the same for somebody."

"I know you would. I don't care about the money. Stop saying I care about the money."

You just care about controlling me, she thought. She was exhausted. "I suppose you're going to pay the phone bill? Do you want my forty-two dollars? I'm quite willing to contribute that."

"I'll pay it. I don't want your forty-two dollars. It's just the principle of not spending more than you can afford."

"I never heard of that principle before. Thank you for enlightening me," she said with heavy sarcasm. She stalked off to the bedroom sofa to read. She still felt guilt—perhaps he had become a more unpleasant person because of his pain over her.

Day passed after day. She was ashamed to see anyone, sure that her failure would show, sure that people would laugh at her for her failure. "Poor Brenda. Of course it couldn't work. How did she ever get so obsessed with that crazy suicide caller?" They would feel that the failure justified, retroactively, their contempt for the relationship.

Of course she told Dolly, who tried to play down her indignation at Andy and her relief at the end of the relationship. "She had to rebel against you. She had to pretend that you weren't good in order to justify herself for breaking up. Don't worry about it."

"What if she believes for the rest of her life that I'm a bad person?"

"Don't worry. She doesn't believe that."

"I'll never know that unless she tells me."

"You ought to know that. Brenda, you *have* to start worrying about a job. You have to get away from Ted."

"I know."

She answered ads in the *Washington Post* for writers, writer-editors, and proofreaders. Of course she knew that answering ads in the newspaper was not the best way to get a job, but you had to start somewhere.

Going through the mechanics of job hunting—particularly for jobs that she didn't want anyway—made her feel petty, callous, and counter-revolutionary because the jobs were so far from being radical, but she recognized the necessity of getting away from Ted. If only she were looking for a job in the belief that what she earned would somehow help Andy or enable her to live with Andy, she would have felt cleaner about it, even enthusiastic. Feminist though she supposedly was, the idea of supporting herself simply for the sake of supporting herself seemed meaningless.

One afternoon while Brenda was working on the newspaper's accounts with bookstores, the phone rang.

"Hello . . . "

"Hello there. Guess who this is."

"Hello! How good to hear your voice."

"You'll never learn. I just called because I wanted to know if you're still there."

There were two possible meanings to this, Brenda thought. Either she's worried that I might have done away with myself or she's asking whether I am still here waiting for her. The second may be less probable, but I'll hope it's true. "Of course, I'm still here. I'll always be here. Just in case somebody happened to need me."

"Good." Nervous laughter. "I got your letter."

In fact, she must have had it for about a week.

"Yes?"

"You did make some points. I don't mean that you changed my mind, but you did make some points. Of course I know you aren't a bad person."

"You don't hate me?"

"Hate you? I couldn't ever hate *you.*"

"I still love you very much."

"You would."

"Of course I would—and will. Do you think we can be friends?"

"Friends? I don't. But I guess I'll call again sometime."

Andy called about a week after her previous call. Again, she simply asked how Brenda was doing.

The same day, Brenda wrote a letter.

Dear Andy, (better keep the greeting unromantic, she thought)
I am so glad that you're doing well and that we're speaking again.
Things are not too wonderful here. My job at the paper ends in the beginning of February: it's another woman's turn. I haven't come close to finding another job yet. The atmosphere at the paper is terrible.
All in all, it sounds like a good time to leave town. I might as well look for a job in Cleveland as anywhere else. What do you think of that?

I'd like to be friends with you. In fact, that's a very important goal for me. Maybe if I live in the area, we could see each other in a casual, friendly way.

Now don't react to this too quickly. I'm really not a ravenous sexual monster. I am fond of you in many ways. I think friendship might work very well. I've spent most of my life celibate, and have no objections to that kind of life. I'm sure there's some feminist activity there that I could join.

Take care. I hope you are well.

Love,
Bad

18

It was Thursday, and Brenda and Nina and Dolly had gone out to dinner before the meeting. They were so nervous about the meeting that they could hardly eat. Brenda was choking and coughing with a deep chest cold.

When they walked back into the office, several women were sitting there crying. Leslie said, "Angela killed herself." Angela was a woman who belonged to a group that had worked a great deal with the newspaper in the last six months. She was a quiet woman: none of them knew her well, but the impact of a twenty-four-year-old woman killing herself hit them all.

They sat there for hours. Instead of meeting, they discussed how it happened—hanging—how it could have happened, what they thought Angela had been like. Long pauses intervened between bouts of speech. Some cried. Some said how horrible it was that anyone could die that young. They suspended their anger at one another.

Brenda felt separate. So they did have feelings. Suicide had an impact, but they had to have seen a person's face. It was strange—they knew Angela so little. Angela seemed such a shadowy figure to Brenda, much more shadowy than Andy, even than Andy's first letter. How strange what moved people and what did not. Why couldn't they have acted this way about Andy? How much Brenda would have loved them if they had. But this way . . . it was almost as if they were saying that Angela had been a more real person than Andy, more important, because they had been to a few meetings with her.

Actually, Brenda's first thought had not been of Andy. The moment she heard the words "Angela killed herself," she thought, "I'm surprised it wasn't me." She was surprised. The thought had hovered around her since Andy's Christmas letter.

She felt so full of pain about Andy that she couldn't hold any more. Angela's death ran over her surface like water on a full glass. She cried with the others, but not for the same reason.

When Nina left her at her doorstep at ten-thirty—Nina had driven Brenda home from almost every meeting in the past two-and-a-half years—she sagged up the stairs and into her apartment house. She checked her mailbox and found a letter from Andy. The letter was thick and the handwriting looked ominously agitated.

Fortunately, Ted wasn't home. She fed Mouse and sat on the living room sofa to read it.

Dear Bad,

No, no, no. You can't come here. I have to tell you something that I thought maybe I wouldn't have to. I tried not to tell you.

Bad, I've decided to go straight. I didn't want to do it, but it was the only way. The pain was too bad—nothing was working. So in December I tried thinking about men. I almost hoped it wouldn't work, but it did. The pains and nightmares went away.

Shirl helped me decide. I was really surprised that she did so much—even pushed me to decide. She said I couldn't stay on the fence, not knowing what I was, that I had to make a decision.

It's weird. I went to her because she was a lesbian. But she thought the other was okay. She pushed me to go out with men—even introduced me to some. I never heard of a shrink doing anything like that before.

I've also seen more of a friend of mine—maybe you remember my mentioning him before? Al. He's a good person, calm and has been very helpful. He's a doctor. My folks like him. He's tried for years to get me to go out with him, so I did.

I don't have any more pains, hallucinations, or nightmares and that's all I care about. I'm not too crazy about men or being straight, but I do want to be sane. Nothing is worth the pain I went through. I'm going to stay this way for the rest of my life. I know you'll be angry at me, but that's what I have to do.

Don't try to keep in touch. You're a good person, Bad. You've done a lot for me. But you just can't be part of my life. Go find a life of your own. I hope you'll be happy.

I'm sorry it had to be this way.

Andy

I'm going to kill myself. I said I'd do that if Andy went straight, and I will. I don't want to think about her with a man. If I live, I'll have to think about her with a man. That's too painful.

She literally felt a pain in her vagina. Her chest choked, and her breath, slower because of the cold, felt as if it had stopped on its own without any unnatural intervention.

Brenda went to the bathroom and looked at her bottle of Sominex. Only two left. She put on a jacket and walked to the Seven-Eleven on the corner. She immediately went to the medicine section, picked up a bottle of sleeping pills, took them to the counter, and bought them. Her one regret was that people on the newspaper would think she was imitating Angela, when she would have acted the same if this letter had arrived any other evening.

She returned home and opened her package. Brenda had always thought that she would leave a long letter if she killed herself, but now she did not want to write.

My lover went straight. Left me for a man or men. That was too shameful to write about.

She swallowed pills, two at a time. Mouse, you'll belong to Ted. He'll feed you well, anyway. Sorry, Mouse. Two. Four. Six. Eight. Her hand stalled. She was afraid. These would make her groggy enough to take the others, groggy enough to be unafraid. She went to the refrigerator and got a bottle of wine to wash down the next dose of pills. She went in the bedroom to lie down on her sofa bed and try to get groggy.

Her feet and arms felt numb. Here she was on the sofa where she had made love to Andy—on the phone. Here she had answered Andy's suicide calls.

You'll never answer any more suicide calls. If some other woman had a message, you won't be there. Hypocrite. You told Andy that suicide was wrong.

She felt more and more numb.

Do you want other lesbians to do this if their lovers go straight?

Live, damn you. Don't be ashamed to do what you want other women to do. Pick up the phone and get help. You can't trust yourself not to take more pills unless somebody comes. Wait. Be *sure* you mean to live. Do *not* call unless you will live. Do not display any uncertainty or ask to be begged to live. Okay, do you have the courage of your cowardice? Who? Dolly. But she's straight. She won't understand. Nina? No, she's got enough problems, don't let her know.

She dialed Dolly's number.

"Hello." Dolly sounded tired.

"Dolly." Her voice shrieked. "She's gone *straight. Straight.* I got a letter saying Andy's gone straight." She summoned a little more control. "I'm sorry. I'm sure you're tired after that meeting. I've taken some pills. Just eight Sominex. I should be okay. But I really feel weird and I want somebody here. *Don't* worry. I am absolutely *not* going to kill myself. Could you come over?"

"Of course. Go drink some Coke. Don't go to sleep. Walk around. I'll be there as soon as I can."

"Thank you so much."

She felt thankful that there was a woman she could lean on. A woman would be there. Brenda didn't think. She stumbled to the refrigerator, got a Coke, and drank a swig.

She walked across the living room, sitting down sometimes. Mouse mewed and she stroked him behind the ears. "I'm all right, Mouse," she said aloud. "Don't worry. We'll stay together."

A woman was coming to take care of her and that was all that mattered at the moment. Her life seemed horrible, but a woman would stay there for a night. Woman. She wanted to be mothered, enfolded. She lay down a few times, though she forced herself to keep awake.

It took Dolly about forty-five minutes to drive over from Virginia. Dolly arrived and hugged her.

"Thanks so much. Seeing you is good." She felt too weak to talk or cry. There was a great buzzing in her ears.

"Did you drink a Coke?"

"Yes, but I want to sleep. Can I sleep?"

"I guess so. Is there a place I can sleep?"

"Yes, on the bed."

Dolly lay on the old canopy bed and Brenda on her sofa bed. She could almost cry because there finally was a woman in her home, spending the night with her. Dolly's presence changed the feeling of the whole apartment.

Brenda's racking cough woke her early in spite of the pills. Her body still felt numb and her ears still rang.

"We'll take care of that. I'll have Nina get you some medicine. I need to go home for awhile, so maybe she can be with you."

"No, don't call her."

"Of course I have to call her. She's your friend—she'll want to know. I'll just wait until 7:30, then I'll call."

"I don't want anybody to know—a fake suicide attempt—how embarrassing. Don't tell."

"I have to tell Nina. How are you doing?" Dolly got her a Coke and was making some tea for herself.

"I don't want to live. I will, but I don't want to. I don't want to think. I don't feel that there's much to live for, if the woman I love

and who loved me can be forced by electric shocks to go to a man."
Her voice shook. "I don't know whether you can understand, but
it's just too terrible."

"That's selfish! You have to live! Your friends need you! The
paper needs you."

"Oh, I won't. You know damn well I won't. But I don't *want* to
live. I will, but I feel like hell. I'll try to think of my friends. I feel a
little spacey anyway."

"That's okay, you'll be all right. Think of Andy."

"Oh, God, I'm trying not to."

"She doesn't want you to die. She won't stay straight. One thing
all this has showed me is how hard people cling to their sexual
identities. She'll go back someday."

"I hope so. I really hope so. Even if it isn't with me. I don't care if
it's with goddamn Eileen, just so it's a woman."

"Of course she will. She's a lesbian. I'm sure of that."

"Thanks."

"I do think I should call Nina. I need to go home and get some
things and I don't want you to be alone."

"Thanks. I mean, don't worry, I won't do away with myself. But I
don't feel too eager to be alone." She groaned at the thought of the
other collective members living in Nina's group house hearing
about her.

Dolly left the room and soon returned. "Nina's coming. She'll
bring some cough medicine. I'll stay until she arrives."

Nina arrived, hugged her, and brought a brown bag full of syrups
and lozenges.

"Oh, Brenda Anne."

"It's all right, I'm okay. Just miserable, a little sick, and a little em-
barrassed. I'm going to the office soon."

"The office! No, you don't have to go to the office."

"I want to go. I'll feel better if I go there and work. It'll occupy
my mind."

On Sunday morning she began her letter.

Dearest Andy,
    You know, of course, that I am sorry, terribly sorry that things
worked out this way, but it doesn't change how brave you have been.
You have undergone far worse tortures than most people ever know.
Who knows what she would do under those circumstances?
    I know that I love you very much, no matter what you do. Nothing
can change that. This has been the finest moment in my life, and it

has made me unshakably lesbian. I might have found it much harder
to leave Ted otherwise.

I want you to know that I will still do anything for you, *anything*
that you might ever need.

Part of me will always wish, no matter how far-fetched that is.
Maybe when we are old we can be in a nursing home together as we
had planned. I know I'll still care. Don't ever be afraid to communi-
cate with me if you want to. Even if you have been married or whatev-
er, don't hesitate. Nothing will change how I feel.

You're the dearest woman I've ever known.

Love always,
Bad

I can't let her know about the suicide attempt, Brenda decided.
She couldn't handle that. Maybe someday if we get back together
I'll tell her about it.

When Brenda walked down the street, she was defeated, as if
each man she passed could see what had happened and was laugh-
ing at her. She had been less afraid of them: she had felt, "Nothing
you do can touch me because a wonderful woman loves me." Now,
she felt that they had won, they had stolen away Andy.

Two other women took the office job in February when Dolly
and Brenda's terms expired. Theoretically, she believed in the
principle of rotation of offices and feared the creation of a move-
ment bureaucracy. This theory was based on her realization that
she herself would cling to any paid movement job she could get for
as long as possible: she expected others to have the same inclina-
tion.

Moving out of the office job was one of the hardest things Brenda
ever did. She had nothing but the newspaper, nothing that mat-
tered, she felt.

Nobody would keep the books as conscientiously as she did.
Nobody would enter the checks as quickly. Nobody would keep as
close a watch on the cash flow. Nobody would answer letters as
well. Nobody would be as good on the telephone. She trained the
other women in office procedures as thoroughly as possible. In a
week, they said she was doing too much work and not giving them a
chance to become independent, so she had to stay home and job
hunt.

One afternoon while Brenda was making job calls, the telephone
rang—as telephones so often do.

"Hello?" The voice was Andy's.

Brenda tried to find a way to speak calmly and sweetly and to hide how she really felt.

"How are you?"

"Home with a cold again—you know the kid. I've had more colds this year . . . How are *you*?"

"Surviving."

"Good. You got my letter?"

"Yes. I've written you a reply."

"I'll bet. I'm almost afraid to open it."

"It's a gentle reply."

"It *is*?"

"Yes, I just said that I'd always care about you no matter what you did. Period. You've been through a lot."

"Bad, you are something else. I can't believe how good you are." Her voice was incredibly warm given the circumstances. Brenda was almost angry that the voice sounded so affectionate.

"I can't believe it either." Her tone was slightly dry. "I don't feel great. I feel lousy. But I love you—you should know that."

"I do know it. I'm sorry. I never thought this would happen."

"I didn't believe it either."

"It's all crazy. I don't think I could ever really want to be straight. Imagine—straight-arrow me—ha."

"Ha. Do take care of yourself. Don't do too many silly things."

"Uh-huh. Well, I guess I've got to go. I just wanted to make sure you were all right."

"Thanks."

She just wanted to make sure I'm all right—so she calls five days after I get the letter. I could have been dead five days.

So she sounds apologetic, sympathetic, almost tender. You damn fool, of course she'll keep calling. She'll never stop calling. She'll go through ten more changes. She isn't worth dying for. It was crazy to think of killing myself over somebody so changeable.

Perversely, Brenda was comforted by this recitation. "She'll never stop calling" was a particularly appealing phrase.

A few days later a letter arrived.

Darling Bad,
    I'll never write another letter like this. I'll never be able to feel this way about a man. Ugh!
    I just have to let you know that I still love you. As much as ever. More. I was wrong when I thought I stopped loving you. I really did think it. Shirl said it was true. But it wasn't.

I love everything about you. You're so good, so gentle. You're so sexy. I can't let myself think about that. You don't know how much it hurts not to be able to think of that.

I've been crying. I'm crying while I write this. I'll never love anybody the way I love you—not even close. When I think of how I've treated you, I just cry. I wish we could have spent a lifetime together.

If it was just a matter of trying hard, I'd try again and again. I'd keep going to shrinks for years to try to get back my sexuality. But the pain was too much—I just couldn't stand the pain.

I'm never going to get married. I won't pretend to care about one man. It could never be like being with a woman. I promise you I'll never love anybody. I'll just go with lots of them and play games.

I don't want to talk about that. I want to tell you how much I love you, how much I wish I could touch you, kiss your breasts and your clit. It frightens me to think about it and write about it, but I *have* to let you know one last time how I feel.

Your Andy *loves* you. You can remember that always. Even if you never hear from me, remember that. I wish there was some other life where we could be together.

Your Andy

Of course Brenda cried. She put the letter in a special drawer with Andy's pictures and locks of hair.

Vindication. She wasn't so awful after all.

The next time Andy called, Brenda was hoping to continue the tone of affection.

"Your letter was beautiful. Thank you for telling me you love me."

"Yes, I love you—that doesn't do you much good."

"It does a lot of good."

"I'm glad. It makes me feel horrible. *The Children's Hour* is playing in a theater in town and I sat through it three times and cried. What's the point of living if I can't be with the woman I love? I might as well die."

You feel like killing yourself. A surge of anger accompanied the usual pain Brenda felt when Andy spoke of suicide. You're the one who left me.

"Don't say that, Andy. Don't do it."

"Why not? I don't like being around men. I go out with one and then another and I feel so cold that I think I could be a prostitute or something. That way I could rip them off."

"That doesn't sound like you. I don't believe you really want to do that."

"Of course I don't want to, but I can't do what I want to do—be with you. I'm a traitor. I don't want to be a traitor. My wanting to kill myself has usually been at times when I've betrayed gays. Why should I live as a traitor for the rest of my life? I know better."

Good God, now do I have to soothe her into being a heterosexual? Tell her it's all right? Maybe I'd just as soon she died. Let her die if I can't have her. Let her die rather than belong to the Man. She is a traitor, that's the truth.

Brenda felt anger and weariness coursing through her. She was a little horrified that she was tempted to say, "Go ahead, then. Die." She was tired of feeling powerless. If this was the only power she could have with Andy, then why not use it? She'd saved Andy from suicide so many times—or thought she had. If you can give life, can't you take it, too? She had tried to save Andy for women, but if there was no chance?

You really are a devil, she told herself. Try playing God and you wind up being the devil. Of course they are the same thing — totalitarian males seeking hegemony.

"No, baby, that's not the only way. I still think you're fine. You can't be sure how your life will turn out. It's all so unpredictable."

"Huh. I think it is predictable. I won't turn into anything good."

"You could never really be bad. You're so self-critical. At least you usually know when you're doing something that isn't wonderful. Many people never admit that. I think you're a lot better than they are."

"Yeah, I know I'm a traitor. That makes me wonderful. Don't you worry, I'm getting punished for what I've done to you."

19

"You can say being with a man isn't so bad. Maybe it isn't for you. You did it for years. But I'm not really straight, and I hate it. Ugh. I know I'll never like it . . . "

Brenda had never believed that Andy actually had slept with a man yet: she had thought that this "going straight" was more of a theoretical choice, which involved going out for the evening with men and considering what sleeping with them would be like. For the first time, she realized that Andy had chosen men in a more personal way. A pain shot through her body, vagina, chest, and head.

" . . . What's the point of living," Andy went on. "If that's what 'love' is like, it's awful."

Brenda felt part of her chest cave in. Her restraint was gone, suddenly.

"How *could* you? How could you take a substitute like *that* for our beautiful lovemaking? I won't do that ever. I couldn't. I couldn't 'settle,' even with another woman."

"You're angry. I knew that under all that niceness you were really angry."

"Of course I'm angry."

"You don't have anything to be jealous about. I hate it. At least you can remember what it was like when we were together. I can't even let myself think about it because of the shocks."

"I can't think of it either. I think of it, and think of you with a man, and it makes me sick. Having slept with a man myself makes it worse, makes me able to feel it more clearly. Thinking of you with a man gives me pains in my vagina, makes me feel raped, like our lovemaking was invaded. I don't know whether I'll ever be able to sleep with anyone again. Why can't you be celibate like me?"

"I don't know. Shirl told me that I shouldn't do that, that I should try to be one thing or the other."

"God damn Shirl to hell. Don't you have any mind of your own anymore? Why sleep with men if it feels so awful?"

"I don't know. I'm afraid. I want to get away from the pain and the nightmares. *They* can protect me. You can't."

Back to the caveman—via electricity. Man would keep control. The rapist and the protector were one. Trusting muscles was safer than trusting love. She could not protect the woman she loved. The blatancy of the argument struck her.

"But don't you see, they're all in it together. The one who shocked you—and the ones who benefit from it. You're not getting rid of the shock pains, you're submitting to the conditioning. That isn't solving anything."

"You don't know what the pain is like. It was so awful. You don't know how much I wanted to die—how much I still want to die. I can remember more and more details about the shocks. They didn't just put wires on my head, they put them on my genitals, too. I keep wishing I were dead."

Brenda was beyond recall. She had always imagined that they had put wires on Andy's poor genitals, always pictured it that way. It was horrible. No doubt it was more horrible than anything she would ever experience, but, by God, she had her own pains too and needed to speak out. Her voice ran away with itself, choking.

"Listen, I know you've gone through horrible tortures, but you have to listen to somebody else sometimes. You aren't the only person who's ever wanted to kill herself. This whole horrible thing has made me feel that way too. I don't want to live, either, but I will. I don't want to live in a world where my lover can be thrown into the arms of men by some goddamned *machine* and I'm power-less to do anything about it. When I got your letter saying that you had gone straight, I tried to kill myself, but I couldn't go through with it any more than you can. I don't believe in suicide, but you've driven me closer to it than anyone else ever could."

"You tried to kill yourself? No, you didn't! You couldn't have."

"Yes, I took some pills—and then realized that that wasn't what I wanted lesbians whose lovers had gone straight to do. I'm sure now that I'll never kill myself. I didn't mean to tell you, but I just felt that I had to say you didn't have a monopoly on pain."

"You hate me."

"No, I don't. All love has a little hate in it. I'm sure that love is my predominant feeling toward you."

"You'll never forgive me. I should have known you wouldn't."

"You're wrong. I do forgive you. I just had to let the anger out."

"I tried to tell you about the wires and you didn't even listen. You lashed out at me instead," Andy wailed.

"Oh, for God's sake. I know it's horrible. The whole thing's horrible. I always knew they did that to you. Baby, I'm sorry. I've cried, empathized, and brooded about what happened to you as much as I possibly could. Can't you see what's happened to me? You know what it's like to have your lover go straight—it happened to you."

"I know. That's how I know you hate me. I hated her."

"But the circumstances are totally different—totally. I do know that you were tortured. I'm just so worn out. It does hurt."

"When I'm with a man, I think of you, and what you'd think of me. It makes me feel like shit."

"Don't even say that. I don't understand. It reminds me of horrible things. Someone once said that to me before—that black man I went with when I was twenty-two. He married a black woman and told me that he thought of me when he slept with her. You're so totally different—everything between us has been so totally different—and yet you're saying the same thing."

"Oh, no. You think this is the old jive-ass black rip-off of a white woman. I'm not like that. I haven't been like that with you."

"No, no, of course I didn't say that or mean that. Don't be ridiculous. Of course I know you aren't like that. It just frightened me when you said those words. As if I was doomed to live through the same thing over and over again—lying alone, knowing that the person I love is with somebody else. This Al—I hope he *is* black?"

"Yes, he is."

"Thank God, I wouldn't want to trust any white man's feelings about a black woman. The history hasn't been great."

"I date both black and white—my family doesn't care."

"Just so it isn't a woman."

"Yes."

"Oh, damn."

"Maybe I'll get married—I don't know what I'll do. It doesn't matter."

"Now? After all you've been through in the last few months? That's the craziest thing you've ever said. Surely Shirl would persuade you not to do anything that rash?"

"No, she thinks it would be okay."

"She's certainly a great friend to me."

"I know that nothing's been easy for you. I know I haven't done good for you. I knew you'd wind up hating me. That's why Shirl didn't want me to tell you. But I had to go ahead and try."

"Of course you did. I ought to know. I need to know the truth, even if I don't enjoy it. And I do *not* hate you. I love you."

"Sure you do. I've got to get off the phone. I can't take any more of this."

"Okay."

You can't take any more of this.

Brenda lay down on the sofa and choked with sobs.

After Brenda's storm had slightly subsided, she wrote a letter.

Dearest Andy,

I'm sorry that I got so angry, but I've really gone through hell, much worse than you know, and it all poured out. I do love you very much, just as much as ever. Please believe that. Being angry doesn't change that. I still would treat you the same as ever if we could be together. I had wanted to keep how upset I was secret from you, especially to keep my little fling with the pills secret, but holding all that in built up the anger.

I didn't mean to say anything tacky about race. You are *nothing* like the man I mentioned. Just hearing the same words again struck me. The whole situation was strange because I felt very guilty towards his wife and was constantly running around making friends with black women and seeking absolution from them.

I know that I don't always say the right thing about race, but it is hard to know what the right thing is. Is the right thing to confess my every tendency towards racism, or never to mention it? But I know that I can never be perceived without it. I can't expect black people who pass me in the street to see me as neutral, as just a human being, rather than a white. I know that I have to try to overcome the perception of me as white, though, of course, it can never really be overcome. I just have to try to compensate. Of course, I often see color first. The other day when I was riding the bus I suddenly realized that my mind had started registering "woman" first and "black" afterwards when I first see a black woman. It used to be the other way around.

The feminist therapist I've started seeing said the other day that part of the cause of our break-up just had to be racial. (She raised the subject of race; I didn't.) I was pretty annoyed, because I don't think that race was a big factor in our problems. I'll bet you'll be annoyed to hear that she thinks black women are bound to "punish" white women for the racism they've experienced in life. Now, I know I shouldn't tell you this, but I wanted you to know what it feels like to have some shrink you never met dissect you, impute motivations to you, and judge you. And that's exactly how I feel about Shirl.

I can't believe Shirl actually would think it was okay for you to get married now, in a time of so much pain, change, and confusion. After all, heterosexual women don't necessarily force themselves to go out with men about whom they feel ambivalent or push to get married right after breaking up with someone else (or at least feminist ones don't). Don't you think you're pushing all this a bit fast?

Well, damnit, I love you anyway, and I hope that comes across loud and clear.

Much love,
Bad

The doorbell rang. It was the special delivery messenger, of course.

The writing on the envelope was so scrawled that she knew Andy must have been upset when she wrote it. The letter was written on yellow legal sheets from Andy's office. Huge, shaky words flung themselves across the pages. Several brown smears streaked the second page. The first page began with a postscript added near the top of the page, "Don't worry about the blood. I got a nosebleed while I wrote this."

Dear Bad,

I just got your last letter and brought it here to the office to read it. I couldn't believe what I saw. You said you didn't expect black people to see you as a human being. (I kept rereading it to see if you really said that.) We are human. We do see people as human. I'm not a racist. I've had lots of white friends. I take people for what they are.

I should have seen it all along. You are a racist. I can't believe it. I let myself trust you and love you. I *did not* ever punish you because you're white. I don't rip off people like that.

Black men are changing. Al is a real friend, supportive, calm, helpful when I am down (though he doesn't know why).

You say the person who shocked me was a man. He was white! All the women he shocked were black. You say men have hurt me, but white people have hurt me and my people. Black people help each other. My family is good and has helped me a lot. They accept anything anybody does except being gay.

I am black. I am proud to be black. I can't love anybody who doesn't understand that.

There isn't any point to our talking and writing to each other. There isn't any understanding between us. Stop hurting me—I can't stand any more.

Andy

Oh, goddamn letters. She took that remark of mine about not being perceived as a human being totally out of context.

I hurt you—damnit, you're the one who left me. You're the one who went straight. You're the one who betrayed me. If this Al's so great, why do you say sleeping with him is so awful?

You always have to be the one who's hurt most. The injured one.

So now that you've betrayed women, you can be proud to be black. Is that what it's like loving someone who's oppressed three ways? If she betrays one group, she can always go to the other and still be the poor, oppressed one. Why should I believe your blackness goes any deeper than your lesbianism? You were so damned eager to pass for straight. I bet you'd pass for white if you could. It's the same thing. You're a coward, a traitor and a coward. No courage to stand up to your family. I learned to resist my parents. Why couldn't you learn to resist yours? Damnit, I've always seen you as a woman first, a lesbian, a woman like me, and then black. We're more alike than different. So some people would say I was racist because I see your being a lesbian as more important than being black. The Man wouldn't have shocked you if you weren't a lesbian. Why do you think he was so threatened by our getting together?

So an employed black doctor who doesn't know all your suffering and hasn't been through all of the changes you've gone through, who wasn't there for the suicides, the hypnosis, can be calmer than an unemployed woman, dependent on a husband she wants to get away from, who has listened to all your griefs and been rejected by you a dozen times—I'm not surprised. Anybody new would be calmer. You wore me out.

After storming for some little while in grief and anger, Brenda took action—in her usual way, by writing a letter.

Dearest Andy,

I am totally horrified by your interpretation of my letter. Of course I didn't say that black people weren't human or couldn't treat white people in a human way. Please go back and read the letter again.

Can you possibly believe that I'm such a dreadful racist? I love you very much. My greatest desire has been to spend my whole life with a black woman, not because she is black but because she is you.

I never said you were a racist. I don't ever call black people racist for being angry at whites.

Even if I have some racism in me, so do all men in this society have sexism in them. Most of them do not even acknowledge the existence of sexism and would not believe they should fight against it as I feel I should fight against racism. Surely no man you could find would struggle more with his sexism than I with my racism. Couldn't love you more either.

Your Bad

Couldn't she talk to the black man—talk to Al? How could he want a woman sent to him by electric shocks? How could he let the white torturer be his matchmaker?

Goddamnit, Al, black men say they've been castrated? Look at Andy—isn't she the one who's *really* been castrated? They took away her power to sleep with women, the sexuality she'd held for all of her life up to age twenty-seven. What about me? I'm castrated. Can't even touch the woman I love or she'll get shock pains.

How can you go along with that? Be a brother—help us. Don't screw her, don't take advantage of her.

20

Brenda was even angry at Dolly.

They rode together, Dolly driving as always, across the smooth Maryland fields away from the small town printer's where the newspaper was produced.

"Let's go to the next mall," Dolly had said. "I need to buy some things. Okay?"

"Sure." She would go anywhere with Dolly, to be in the soothing presence of a friend. This small insulation made the pain less fierce for a few hours.

The shopping mall was full of boutiques and glass. Women were everywhere. But every one of these women either wore a wedding ring, had hair just styled by the dresser, or led one or more children — or all three (generally, all three symptoms were combined). The clothes were pastel.

The trouble was not that the clothes were pastel—it was that there seemed to be no room for clothes that were not pastel. There was no room for women who did not wear wedding rings. The ring bound suburban culture, and the women hurried and flurried within its grasp, buying baby clothes, new stockings, perfume, the latest style blouse, and monogrammed toilet seat covers.

There was not a breath of politics anywhere—not even liberal politics. Malls are private property: political demonstrations can be banned. If you want to boycott non-union manufacturers or merchants who use mannequins covered with blood to liven up their store windows, don't picket in a mall unless you want to be arrested.

There was nary a political button or poster to be seen.

Worst of all, the people would assume that she was one of them, that she was part of a life that was dedicated to nothing but the family and consumption of material goods. They would think that she belonged to some man, or would belong to one someday. She felt that they wanted to annihilate her. She wished that the words "lesbian feminist" were written all over her.

They did not want to know that she was a lesbian. They wanted to submerge Andy in their ranks. They were submerging Andy in their ranks.

She knew Dolly did not feel the same. When Dolly looked at the young blonde, bouffant wife walking with her little boy, Dolly just worried about whether the woman was under stress and looked for its signs in her face. Brenda saw a woman who was spending her life serving two men: her husband and her son. A woman who would probably be willing to keep other women down for the sake of those men. A woman who probably would deny the reality of Brenda's love for Andy, who would not want to hear that women did those things. An oppressor. She, too, is my oppressor, though she is oppressed herself.

"Oh, those poor women with young children," Dolly exclaimed. "What hard lives they have. We should spend more time trying to reach them."

"I don't feel quite that way. If they want to accept us as we are, then we can speak to them. But I wouldn't work with anybody who wouldn't allow me to be an open lesbian."

"You can't expect that!" Dolly exclaimed in her eager voice. "People won't be that politically advanced right away. You have to meet them on their terms and be nice to them, and then, when they like you, you can let them know you're a lesbian."

Brenda flared up, physically angry. "No. That's putting down lesbians. We have to be who we really are. Saying that we have to pretend is saying that lesbianism is inferior, is something to hide. It's reinforcing everything that forces lesbians to hide. It's undercutting lesbians who try to be open."

"It's arrogant to insist that everyone be politically conscious immediately." Dolly was a little angry, too, though nowhere near as angry as Brenda.

"Arrogant! Jesus Christ. I can't believe you said that. Those women with the babies are my oppressors if they won't let me be myself. They're their own oppressors, too, if they keep down lesbians and prevent women from having the option. They aren't free either if they don't have the choice."

"Those poor women . . . "

"You're my oppressor if you don't want me to be open. 'Those poor women' are reinforcing all of our oppression by accepting the system of male domination and dedicating their lives to individual men. I'll work with them in so far as they refuse to submit to the life that keeps women in slavery."

"People have to start being radicalized somewhere."

"Let them start then."

"You're so arrogant."

"I'm angry. I'm furious. I can hardly stand being this angry at you. Maybe we'd better stop talking about this."

"Okay." Dolly was flushed, too.

Dolly was her support. Being this angry with her hurt sharply. Why was it that even the oppressed—these women, barely able to cope with their children, black men who couldn't find jobs, even many straight black women coping with double oppression—were her oppressors? When would it end? She didn't want to be angry at these people—it made her feel guilty. But she must put lesbians first because no one else did.

21

One day, Brenda received a letter from Andy that was even more frightening in appearance than the one with bloodstains: the handwriting was strikingly different. It was still discernibly Andy's handwriting, but it was utterly different from the handwriting on any other letter she had seen in the past year. The writing was slanted severely backwards, as in classic "introverted" handwriting. Some of the letters were different.

Dear Brenda Anne,

I have so much to say. I know you aren't going to understand or like it, but I have to tell you anyway. I am so happy.

I was feeling so low and miserable. I wanted to die. Then I met this group of people. They are wonderful people, men and women, black and white, old and young, Christians of all backgrounds and Jews. They all believe in Jesus and meet together to praise him. I went to their meetings and told them about my pain. They listened to me and prayed over me.

I prayed as hard as I could. I begged God to forgive me for all my sins. When they were praying and I was praying, a wonderful thing happened to me. God showed me that my lust for women was wrong. I asked him to take it away, and he took it away. He took away the pain too. I cried with joy. Everyone hugged me and was happy for me.

I can touch women now, with no fear. I know that they were meant to be my sisters, not my lovers. The women in this group have shown me what real love between women is, support in being closer to Jesus.

Jesus is real. I have always believed in Him, but not enough. I know that you do not believe in Him and cannot understand the joy I have, but I pray for you and have asked my friends to pray for you that you too may know him and change your life.

I did not see Jesus, but he was with me all along. He saved me from the shocks. He saved me from killing myself. Now I see that and I love Him.

I have given up the old ways and my old name. Andy is dead. I hate the sound of that name. I am a new person. I am Karen.

Our beliefs are so different that I don't think there can be any communication between us, but I love you in a new, pure, Christian way, and I will pray for you. I hope you will find the happiness in Jesus that I have found.

Karen

A rage filled Brenda. She did not shed a tear. This was truly the end.

You traitor. This is too much. Not only a new life but a new ideology to match your life.

So Jesus saved you from suicide, did he? How convenient. That means I didn't. You can pretend that he did what I did. It's much easier to love an abstract person out in the sky than a real person, with real needs and demands, isn't it? His demands can be interpreted by you. Very clever.

Real men disgust you. Making love with them isn't bearable. So you go to a god-man to make them bearable to you. You imagine this perfectly gentle, loving man who doesn't exist, and say of course my real love is for Him and earthly relationships can't be as satisfying. Damn you, how can you con yourself like that?

I should have known that anybody who was looking for a savior sooner or later would find the great savior of them all. I wasn't a perfect savior—I expected something in return. Well, at least you can't drive Jesus to suicide.

Real love between women. How dare you say that? Real love is pushing one another to be straight. Real love is being a madam, handing another woman over to a man, holding her hand and soothing her to make it better. That makes me sick. Damn your "loving friends" who soothe you into bed with a man.

You dare—you dare to pray that I'll get fucked, too. You could at least be squeamish about that idea. Never. No way, baby. Never.

So now I see that enough physical torture can make anybody betray anything. An edifying lesson. I might have learned it from reading about the Moscow trials of the '30's, when Stalin tortured heroes of the revolution into saying they'd always been agents, but you don't really learn from reading, you have to see it in your own life. So now I know that you would betray not only me and your sexuality, but the belief that women have the right to love each other. Perhaps anyone would do the same. It's a beautiful world.

"Andy is dead." You killed her. You killed my precious baby. Karen, you dishonest bitch, you aren't half the woman Andy was despite all her problems.

"Andy has become a Jesus freak," she said, irony in her voice, to her friends.

What was she supposed to do with a heartful of love for a woman who repudiated her as a sinner? It was ludicrous. There was no way of expressing her love.

One day Brenda wanted to masturbate.

She had not touched herself sexually since meeting Andy. She had been so intoxicated by Andy's touch that masturbation seemed unromantic and ridiculous. She had no desire to try it. Then, when her lover was unable even to think about sex, feeling shock pains at the mere thought of women, any sort of preoccupation with Brenda's own body would have seemed gross. When she had heard that Andy had gone straight, everything physical seemed nauseating.

Now, she might as well do it. She did have a sexuality independent of that damned Jesus freak.

The idea frightened her a little. She was terrified of being overwhelmed by memories of Andy, of crying uncontrollably.

No, damnit, she was independent. Brenda propelled herself to the bedroom and lay down on her couch-bed. Quietly, she masturbated through a small orgasm, not letting herself think of Andy. A sense of relief passed through her. She had survived.

Within a few minutes, the telephone rang.

"Hello?"

"Hello," said a feeble voice. "Are you still speaking to me?"

"Yes. How are you?" Brenda's voice was incredibly calm—if a voice could be poised, hers was.

"Not so great. I don't know if you care, but I thought I'd tell you. I started having the most awful pain last night. My grandmother had to take me to the hospital in the middle of the night. It was appendicitis."

"Good grief, are you all right."

"I guess so. They cut my appendix out, but it had ruptured, so the scene was pretty heavy."

"What hospital?"

"Fenwick General."

"How are you feeling?"

"I'm pretty weak. Maybe it's crazy calling you."

"No, no, I'm glad you did. I want to know."

"You really do?"

"Do you want me to come there? I will if you want."

"I don't know. Not yet."

"Okay, baby. Whatever you say. Get some rest."

"Yes, Bad."

Brenda hung up the phone, crying and shaking with excitement. "Not yet!" That was the most favorable response she had heard in six months to the idea of going to Cleveland.

Brenda hurried down Connecticut Avenue to the nearest florist, less than two blocks away. She had wanted to send Andy spring flowers: it had positively hurt seeing the first daffodils and not being able to send her any.

I will go there, Brenda told herself. I don't care whether she gives me permission or not. I don't care whether she rejects me. Nothing can be worse than what I've gone through already. (Not even seeing Al? What if I run into Al?)

22

Brenda woke early Sunday morning and called Andy. People in hospitals couldn't sleep late.

There was no answer.

Perhaps they moved her room. Brenda called Cleveland information and got the central number for Fenwick General.

"Hello. Could I please speak to Karen Carpenter? I called her room, 511C, just now and she wasn't there. Has she changed rooms?"

"Karen Carpenter? She had a relapse last night and is in intensive care. You can't speak to her there."

The voice switched her.

"Intensive Care."

"Hello. I'd like to find out about Karen Carpenter. How is she doing?"

"Are you a member of the family?"

Sexist, heterosexist family-ideologist, she cursed, hoping she would not be caught. "Yes, I'm her cousin Brenda. How is she?" How dare you not recognize any other relationship.

"She's had a bad time, but we think she's pulling through."

"Can I talk to her?"

"No."

"Will you give her a message?"

"In a while, when she's able to hear it."

"Please tell her Cousin Brenda sends her love. We're close. I think she'd want to hear it."

"All right."

Let's hope the nurse doesn't mention Cousin Brenda to other members of the family. Selfish idiot, she yelled at herself. So glad to have her in the hospital and wanting you—not even thinking how dangerous it might be.

She kept calling through the rest of the day.

At two o'clock, her phone rang.

"Hello there, Cousin Brenda."

"Baby, are you all right?"

"Yes, honey, I'm okay."

"Thank goodness. What happened?"

"Internal bleeding. I guess my blood doesn't coagulate very well after all the anti-coagulants I took for the clot. Something like that."

"You're okay now?"

"Yes, honey, don't worry. I'll be just fine. I asked the nurse if I could take your beautiful yellow flowers to intensive care. She thought I was crazy."

"You are, silly."

"What about you, Cousin Brenda? I thought it was so sweet to get a message from my loving cousin."

"They didn't want to say anything to me unless I was a member of the family. I was worried that cousin was too distant a relationship, but I was afraid to say 'sister' in case they knew you didn't have one."

"They say when you're on the critical list you can only see and get calls from members of your family."

"Would that be a problem if I visited you. I might have trouble passing?"

"Don't worry about that. I could tell them I wanted to see you."

"So should I come?"

"Not yet."

On Monday morning, she began calling Cleveland's women's groups, asking if they knew where she could spend the night. One woman said that there was a new women's shelter that sometimes had room for out-of-town visitors. She called the shelter, and did not disdain to mention that she was on the newspaper. The woman at the other end of the line enthusiastically assured her that there was room, for five dollars a night if she could afford it.

Brenda purchased an amethyst cross. She wrote a note to enclose in the gift box, saying, "May this lavender cross symbolize the fact that it is possible to be both Christian and gay." I'm not both, of course, but it is possible.

She would do any damn thing Andy wanted. If she was still enthusing about Jesus, fine, Brenda liked Jesus too, though she didn't believe he was god. If Andy wanted someone to pray with, Brenda would go down on her knees and pray with her. True, that was an abandonment of her principle that religion was a basically destructive force that ought to be challenged, but an individual was more important than a principle.

Proudly, she boarded the Greyhound for Cleveland. The tie between them was stronger than anything. Andy still found her irresistible. Being sick made Andy realize how much she needed Bad. No matter what happened, they would continue to be linked together—so went her thoughts for the entire journey.

As soon as the hospital began accepting calls the next morning, Brenda called Andy.

"Hello."

"Hello. And where were you last night? You're getting wicked, Bad. I called until after midnight and you weren't there."

"I'm at a women's shelter."

"And who are you sheltering there?"

"Myself. And I'm not there. I'm here. In Cleveland."

"Bad! You're in Cleveland! You didn't!" Her voice, fortunately, wasn't really horrified.

"Yes. I thought you were implying that I could come."

"Sure, it's okay. Since you're here, you might as well come over." She described the rather complicated bus route to Brenda.

Brenda took the bus back into downtown Cleveland, then boarded a bus for Fenwick.

As she left the city and approached Fenwick, the road changed. Residential areas with simulated Tudor homes relieved her eyes.

Fenwick itself had a small main street (on the bus route), lined with small brick colonial-style stores. These, too, are Andy's streets, she told herself. When she left the main street, she passed nothing but two-story houses with crocuses and hyacinths beginning to bloom in the gardens. Andy lived in a good neighborhood: of course she does. I mustn't be patronizing.

Brenda rehearsed conversations, becoming a little tense as she approached the meeting. She had put on the gold ring again, debating at length whether to wear it on the left hand as a wedding ring or whether Andy might consider that too pushy since they had broken up. Brenda decided on the right hand.

She wore an old green corduroy suit that Andy had often seen and a black turtleneck. Did the circles under her eyes make her look less pretty?

It had been seven months, almost to the day, since she had last seen Andy. The winter had been long, but at last it was giving way to a new spring.

Fenwick General was a rather small, red brick building, fairly attractive as hospitals go.

She asked directions, worried that someone would challenge her because she wasn't family.

Brenda walked down the fifth-floor corridor and through the double doors. The first room on the right was 511C. She turned in and tried to smile.

It was a double room. A young white woman slept in the first bed. Beyond that hung a curtain.

She walked across the room, past the curtain.

Andy lay on the bed, grinning.

They were both much thinner now, almost gaunt. Cheekbones stared out of both faces. Brenda had lost almost twenty pounds and estimated that Andy's loss was similar. Dark circles stretched under two pairs of eyes.

Brenda wanted to rush across the room and kiss her, but was afraid.

There was a pause for a moment.

"Why did you come here?" The voice was cheerful, but absolutely cold.

The cold invaded Brenda. No words came from her. She was terrified.

"Did you come here to see if I was alive? I'm alive. Did you come here to see if I was well? I'm well." She sat up further in the bed. "Now you've seen me with your own eyes. You might as well go."

Brenda turned quickly to the window and stared out at the rooftops of other levels of the building. She did not want to cry. Be strong. What would Katherine Hepburn do in this situation? Tears formed in her eyes in spite of herself.

"What did you expect?" asked Andy. "More? You're crazy. There isn't any more. What did you expect? Tell me. Why did you come?"

Brenda forced herself to turn back to Andy—or to whoever it was who was inhabiting Andy's body.

"I love you. Why else would I come?"

"Don't you know I've changed?" Andy chuckled. "I'm not like that any more."

"I always tried to keep up with your various changes. I have a present for you." Her voice was very shaky. She dived into her purse.

"A present. Why?"

"Because you're in the hospital." She handed the box to Andy.

"I don't think you should be giving me presents. Save your money."

"Open it."

Andy found the cross and the note. She chuckled. "It's pretty. But you shouldn't have. You never give up."

"No, I never give up on you. I'd follow you anywhere. I'll pray with you if you want. I'll pray for us to be brought back together."

"You? I know what you think. You don't believe in God." Andy made a gesture showing Brenda a book purporting to be written by Billy Graham.

"I don't know whether God exists or not, but I do believe in trying to be as good as possible, and I'm willing to admit my faults and repent them. Whatever is important to you is important to me."

"I know there's a God. He's changed me. He took away the pain. No human being could do that."

"I believe that you did that yourself, that you got in touch with some deeper part of yourself."

"I did it myself?" Andy laughed. "I don't buy that. If I could do that, I would have done it a long time ago."

"Maybe you weren't ready."

"I wasn't ready for Jesus. I hadn't repented. I hadn't given up the old me. I'm the new me, now," she exclaimed in an outburst of forced, overstated joy.

"The old you was a good person, too."

"No, she wasn't. I know you think that, but I'm glad to get rid of her. You don't want to know the new me. Maybe you should go away."

"I suppose I believe that the old you is still within you somewhere."

"And you're going to unearth her?" Andy laughed at her. "No way. You've come all this distance for nothing."

"You asked me to come."

"I was weak. I thought you might as well see that I was okay so you wouldn't worry about me. You've seen me. But I won't give up Jesus."

"I'm not asking you to give up Jesus."

"Yes, you are."

"Jesus believed in love. I don't know if there's a God, but I do know that the only God worth believing in is one that does not oppose human beings' love. Faith and hope are all very well, but the greatest of them is love. Corinthians. There isn't any evidence to the contrary in the Gospels. Oh hell, you've read all the books about gays and the church. Why should I have to say that to you?"

"Jesus didn't cure me until I repented. That was what He wanted. I believe. I'm happier than I've ever been. *Ever.*"

"You don't sound happier. Your voice sounds forced."

"I'm *happy*. This is a better life. I'll never go back."

"I'm sorry—for you."

"Don't be. I'm cured." She kept on grinning and speaking in a cheerful, totally unpleasant tone. "I'm strong."

Andy jumped out of bed and tried very shakily to bounce around the room. "I am strong, I am invincible, I am woman," she half-sang, half-shouted at Brenda. "See, I don't need you."

The song was now poisoned. Yes, damnit, she was still woman, but at some point a woman injured other women so much that she lost the right to count herself as part of the movement, Brenda thought angrily. Or did she? Andy had suffered so much. But surely the point is not "I am woman"—no one person is Woman—but "we are women"? How can you be part of the movement unless you are working with other women, trying to help other women? You're still oppressed, though, even if you're a traitor to your class.

Andy got back in bed.

A nurse walked in. She was a young white woman, very straight-looking, with bouffant hair.

"Excuse me, but I need to take your temperature and blood pressure."

"Of *course*." Andy used her warm voice, full of charm. "How are you, dear?"

"Fine. How are you doing?"

"Couldn't be better. Why, I just love this hospital and all of these sweet folks. I wish I had another appendix so I could come back and have that taken out too."

Andy and the nurse laughed. The nurse put a thermometer in Andy's mouth.

When she took the instrument out, Andy said, "You're the best temperature-taker I've ever met. Are you just as good at checking blood pressure?"

"I hope so, Miss Carpenter."

"Call me Karen. I'm not missing anything—except that old appendix."

"You still have a temperature of 100.5 degrees. Don't overdo, Karen." She wrapped her arm with the device to measure blood pressure.

"Overdo? Me? Never. I get it when I can, but I never overdo."

The nurse laughed. Brenda was ready to vomit.

"Your blood pressure is still high."

"You'll just have to send more of those cute doctors around to keep my blood pressure normal."

Andy and the nurse laughed. (This was an example of that beautiful friendship between straight women, no doubt.)

The nurse got ready to leave.

"Good-bye, sweetie. See you later. If you can't be good, be careful."

Brenda was truly nauseated at that smugness. It didn't sound like Andy.

"Now, what were we saying," Andy inquired, returning to the cold, but cheerful voice.

"You have a temperature. Do you want some water?"

"Okay, sure. I can get it." She made a gesture toward getting out of bed.

"No, don't be silly, I'll get it." She fetched a glass of water. "Do you want a cold cloth for your forehead or anything?"

"No, I'm okay. Never better."

"Uh huh."

An orderly wheeled in Andy's lunch. Andy and the young Asian American woman exchanged friendly hellos.

"You're eating now? Good." Brenda tried to sound neutral and calm.

"Sure, I started yesterday. Mind if I eat in front of you?"

"Of course not. Please go ahead. Anything I can do?"

"Can't think of anything. Look, macaroni and cheese. Oh, wow." She made a grimace.

"Here's the menu for tomorrow. I'll check off what you want. Okay?"

"Sure—if you want to." She began talking in a natural voice without the extra cheer.

"Okay, when we finish this I'll get a Coke."

"Cigarettes, too?" There was a bit of the con in her voice.

"No."

"What are they supposed to do to me?"

"When you're lying in a hospital bed and just got off the critical list yesterday? No way. What about tomorrow's lunch?"

They checked off foods for lunch and dinner. Andy finished eating and Brenda moved her tray away from the bed.

"I have to decide whether I'm still going to testify at the trial even though I've decided not to be gay."

"I hope you'll still testify! It is important. You were right about that."

"You're admitting that I'm right for a change? I never thought I'd see the day."

Brenda flushed. "It's true that I assume I'm always right. Unfortunately, I often am. People don't forgive that easily."

"You weren't right about me."

"Yes, I was. You're a better person than you ever believed. Much better than you believe right now."

"Sure. I don't know what to do about the trial. The Man did do wrong, so the suit is still right. But if I'm not gay, do I need to testify about it?"

Of course. She was afraid to be known as a lesbian.

A black woman of about fifty entered the room. She was pale, heavy, rather tired looking, and very warmly dressed in a heavy coat, wool hat, and scarf.

"Hello, Auntie. This is my Aunt Annie Parker. Aunt Annie, this is Brenda, a friend of mine from D.C. Brenda was in town and she came by to see me."

"Isn't that nice? How do you do?"

"Glad to meet you, Mrs. Parker." They shook hands.

"Will you be here long?"

"I don't know yet."

"She's just passing through," said Andy.

"How are you doing today?" Aunt Annie asked, turning to Andy.

"Fine, just fine."

"I brought you some cookies that your Granny made. Do you feel well enough to eat cookies?"

"Yes, ma'am!"

Like families everywhere, they talked on about nothing. Brenda sensed—perhaps incorrectly, she admitted—that Aunt Annie knew exactly who she was. Andy needed more water and Aunt Annie rushed to get it, not letting Brenda. Eventually, the young woman in the next bed woke and briefly joined their discussion.

Oh, it was crazy having to listen to this when she hadn't seen Andy in seven months and might never see her again. She tried not to cry.

"My, your friend is quiet," Aunt Annie said at one point. "It was so nice of you to stop by and see Karen, Brenda."

"I wanted to, ma'am. I'm always happy to see Karen."

After about an hour and a half, Aunt Annie rose to go. "I must be going. I don't want to tire you out, Karen." The hint that Brenda should leave too was none too subtle.

Brenda remained rooted to her place. "Good-bye, Mrs. Parker. It was good to meet you."

"It was a pleasure to meet you, Brenda, I always enjoy meeting Karen's friends. Don't you have a good friend, Karen, to stay here so long?"

"Yes, ma'am. Bye-bye."

After a moment, Brenda said, "I think she was trying to outlast me."

"Maybe. I don't know."

"Are you tired? Do you want me to leave?"

"No, I'm okay. I'm fine. I told you I was fine. I'm just fine in every way. Can't wait to move on. Yes, there are a lot of things to do and places to go. Maybe I'll move out of this city. Move somewhere more exciting. This place is a little slow. Don't want to cramp my style. I've heard about a computer programming course. Maybe I should take that. Earn more money for a change." Her voice was chipper and cold.

"That sounds pretty dull compared with your present job."

"So what? I could use more money. I'm tired of having so little. I don't want to be a sucker all my life."

"Stop it! You don't sound like yourself at all. It isn't possible that you could have become so cold and hard. You can cut out this obnoxious performance right now. I'm not falling for it."

"Performance? That's what you'd like to believe. This is the new me, this is what I want to be."

"The new you. Well, it's anything but spiritual. It's the opposite. You're coming across as a person who doesn't believe in anything."

"Oh, I believe in something all right. Being careful. Taking care of myself."

"That isn't exactly what Jesus taught. If you care."

"I won't listen to you. You don't believe in Him. I do."

"I know you've suffered and you want to escape more suffering. I understand. But you can't do that by becoming the person you are today. You aren't really cold. The real you must be there underneath, being suppressed."

"Wanting you, you mean? I don't want you. I don't feel a thing for you. The real me is not suppressed. You just can't believe I don't want you anymore. Now I've seen you and I know—I don't."

The telephone rang. Andy picked it up. "Aunt Linda! Aren't you sweet to call! I'm doing just fine. You are? That's sweet. I can't wait to see you. Bye now."

"My Aunt Linda is coming over to see me."

Brenda's anger was competing with her pain. Might as well get angry. You've lost her for good. So what if she's an invalid: she's doing everything she can to torture you. You have to fight back. "You could have kept her away. I'm sick of your family. Why should I have to stand here listening to them when I haven't seen you in seven months? They saw you yesterday."

"You're racist. You don't want to see my family."

"Damnit, how dare you say that. I've wanted to meet your family ever since we became involved. You were the one who didn't want me to meet them because that might jeopardize your closet. Some closet, when you lived with a woman for five years. I'm sure your family knows all about you. Of course I don't want to have to be polite to strangers when you've announced that this is the last day I'll ever see you."

"My family loves me. They want to see me when I'm in the hospital."

"I, of course, don't give a damn whether I see you in the hospital. I only traveled a few hundred miles to do so. I'm perfectly happy to spend endless hours listening to your family chats, as long as you let me stay and come to see you regularly."

"No. I said no."

"I won't say good-bye to you in front of your family. I'm tired of the way you insult me and then turn around and act sweet the minute someone else enters the room. I can't stop crying the minute another stranger walks in. I'm not like you. I can't turn it on and off like that. Everybody thinks you're so damn sweet."

She advanced toward the bed. "You aren't sweet, you just pretend. Everybody is 'honey' or 'dear' to you. You don't really care about anybody. I'm not as charming as you are. Not as many people find me charming." She knew she was alluding to monogamy and promiscuity. Andy did look upset. Good. "But I do know how to love one person—unfortunately. When I told you I loved you, I really meant it." She saved the worst line for last. "But you never loved me." She didn't believe this, was sure it would hurt because it wasn't true. "Never."

"That's not true. I did." Andy's face was sad. "I do want to be able to care about people. I do want to love someone. I just don't want any more pain."

"You have to care more about the people than about the pain, or you won't really love them." She now felt guilty as well as angry and miserably sad. "Come on, kid. Give it a chance. Give me a chance. Let me come back tomorrow and hang around. You can do it."

"*No.* I mean it. I won't change my mind. Today is the last time I'll ever see you."

"That's too bad, because I love you very much and I always will. I don't believe anybody else will ever love you as much. You know where you can reach me. Good-bye." She picked up her purse and marched out.

At least I made an exit. Was I childish to make an exit? Well, what else could I do, say "Good evening, Karen," in front of another aunt? She walked out of the building, defeated. The rain poured on her. The temperature was under 50 degrees. She had forgotten her umbrella. She shivered and waited for the main street bus. The gold ring was removed from her hand and stuffed into the purse.

Andy was the worst she had ever seen her. Brenda could almost have believed that some demon was inhabiting Andy's body. Karen. Perhaps Andy was dead inside. The machine had made her cold.

After long waits and long bus rides, it was well into evening when she arrived at the shelter.

She soon received a telephone call. "Bad? I had to call to tell you how terrible I feel." The old Andy was speaking. "I couldn't believe that I said all those horrible things to you. I'm sorry. 'What are you doing here?' I hated saying those things, but I kept on doing it."

"You'd been sweet on the phone. You'd wanted me to come."

"I know, I know. But when you were there I was so afraid. Maybe you were right when you said I was suppressing my feelings. I'm so afraid of feeling the pains again, Bad. I just don't want to risk feeling those pains."

"I can understand that."

"I was so cold to you. So awful. But I did want to see you. I hated to see you go. I cried and cried. My Aunt Linda came in and she wondered why I was crying so hard. I let her think it was because I was sick from the operation. I am sick! The things I said to you!"

"It's all right, baby. You're apologizing."

"I had to apologize. You looked so thin and miserable and I kept insulting you. If I had known it would be like that I never would have had you come here. Dragging you all the way to Cleveland to be insulted."

"It was pretty horrible, but I wanted to come and see you. By the time I left, you couldn't have kept me away. Perhaps I should have come months sooner."

"No! I couldn't have handled it sooner. I didn't know I could treat you like that. I've done some shitty things before, but this was the worst."

"You tried to see me. That's what counts. I'm glad you tried. Maybe if we kept trying it would get better."

"You'd let yourself in for another time like that? No, I couldn't stand it. I can't keep treating you like that."

"I'm willing to keep on. I always thought there would be many problems if we saw each other. Of course it would be hard for you not to worry about the pain and associate me with it. I thought you wouldn't want to touch me. I didn't exactly anticipate how it would be, but I knew it wouldn't be smooth. But if we keep on trying . . . "

"No, I can't do that to you again. I'm afraid. I don't think the new me is so great, but it's better than the pain."

"Maybe it is, dear. I don't know. You're the only one who knows that."

"I can't handle it, Bad. I can't treat you right. Please go home tomorrow."

"Don't you think that it might be better now that we've talked about it?"

"No, I'd just be the same. I'm sorry."

Andy should have known that nothing could have kept Brenda from trying again the next day. After seven months' wait, she was going to try at least twice.

She retraced the previous day's route with considerably more apprehension. Andy didn't know she was coming. Perhaps someone she didn't want to see would be there.

She walked into the hospital room. Andy's roommate was awake. They quietly exchanged hellos.

Beyond the veil, Andy was asleep. Brenda sat in the chair, pulled a paperback copy of *The Possessed* out of her purse, and tried to read it (for the fourth time—she read Dostoievsky every few years).

She would sit and wait, like a wife, rather than wake Andy like a stranger. Or a man. A man would have wakened her.

There was a temptation to kiss her while she slept. No, it would be wrong to take a touch that a woman didn't give voluntarily—it would be like rape?

God (pardon the expression), what if men were right and there were times when a woman said no but really wanted to be touched? No, she couldn't believe that, that was against all her feminism. She herself said yes when she meant yes and no when she meant no, and other women must be like her.

What if Andy felt a woman's touch without having to worry about it beforehand? Without thinking about the shocks? Or about sin? Let the "sin" be Brenda's. Wasn't it possible that she might feel the old joy and not the shock pains? Of course, she might feel the pains, and it would be Brenda's fault.

She wanted to touch Andy. How strange to be able to see her in bed asleep and not be able to touch her. How strange to see her sleeping and realize they were no longer sexually connected.

A woman had the absolute right to decide who would touch her. Brenda would not violate that right, though she fought over the question within herself.

The boyfriend of the young woman on the other side of the veil visited her.

"That woman is visiting Karen again," she told him. "I think she's a lesbian who's trying to get Karen. Isn't that disgusting?"

He agreed that it was.

See what I go through for you, Andy? Can't you see? She sat there. Eventually the man left.

She had been sitting there for well over an hour when she realized that Andy was awake and crying with her eyes closed.

"Andy?" she whispered. "Karen? Are you awake?"

Andy cried and didn't speak for a moment. She opened her eyes.

"Why did you have to come again? Wasn't yesterday awful enough?"

"I'm sorry if I did the wrong thing. I love you. I just wanted to try again."

"Give up, Bad. It's over. I won't try again. Can't you see when something's over?"

"No relationship with another person is ever over. At least mine aren't. They just change."

There was silence. Andy kept crying.

"I didn't mean to hurt you by coming here."

"I'm the one who'll hurt you if I talk. How long have you been here?"

"An hour or so."

"Why didn't you wake me?"

"It's nice just being near you."

"You're so patient, so gentle. You've waited so long. I feel terrible treating someone like you this way."

"I've only done what I've wanted to do."

"Well, I've done what I haven't wanted to do."

"I was sitting here thinking about kissing you. Do you think I could?"

"I guess so. I'm supposed to be cured." Her eyes were wide open, terrified. She turned her head away from Brenda. Tears still flowed.

Brenda bent down and kissed her cheek.

Andy responded with a slight shudder and still looked frightened.

"You didn't feel any pain, did you?"

"No."

"Do you think that means we should keep on?"

"No. I won't let myself think that way. Please go away, Bad. Please."

"I want to stay. Or, if I leave now, to come back and keep coming back. I will, dear, unless you tell me not to. I will leave if you really want."

"Go, Bad. Please go. I don't want to go through this. Please go back to D.C."

"If you say so. I don't want to keep doing things against your will. I do love you enough to leave you without another grand exit line. Take care of yourself."

She looked at Andy to see if there was any sign of a change, then walked away. Would a man in this position have seduced Andy? Would he have been right? She'd never know the answer.

The first time she had made love to Andy, Andy had been quiet and crying. But this crying was different. Then, she had not shuddered or begged to be left alone.

The NOW Sexuality Task Force, which was a euphemized task force about and of lesbians, was holding a speak-out on lesbianism.

Brenda was drawn to the speak-out.

The event was held in the basement of an old school. About eight women sat in rows of desks in a large former classroom. She didn't know many NOW women. They were a slightly more respectable set of women, who dressed in somewhat more expensive clothes and often had better paying jobs, such as government jobs. In age, education, and background they were very similar to the radical feminists who wouldn't dream of joining NOW. Brenda wondered what made the difference between a woman who decided to be a radical feminist and one who decided to be a feminist but might be uncomfortable with the idea of radicalism. She felt warmer toward these women than most of the radicals she knew did. If there were no radical organizations around, she would join a reformist one.

Since her own lover had been shocked, all lesbians seemed infinitely precious, vulnerable people. She felt that she would risk her life for any of them. She looked around the room, wanting to know (not carnally) each of them, why she was a lesbian, what loves she had known, and how she was holding up.

Two or three older women looked as if they might have been what had been called butches. A few women had the new faces of teenagers. Most of the women were in their twenties, thirties, or early forties and looked like a group of high school teachers. Only three black women were present, two of them well into middle age. Obviously that was not representative of the real numbers of black lesbians in Washington, D.C.

Various women gave presentations. The tall, angular, thirtyish woman who was the moderator spoke about lesbian and gay history, beginning with Sappho and going through World War II, when Hitler sent thousands of gays to the death camps. They were forced to wear pink triangles as symbols of their deviation. She updated the history through gay civil rights organizations, the Daughters of Bilitis, the Christopher Street march, and the feminist movement.

Another speaker, a middle-aged woman, gave the personal story of her coming out, which, she said, "was a process that took thirteen years. You don't just come out all at once."

A lesbian mother and her lover, both very professional looking—one even had bouffant hair—told how they shared the mother's two children. The mother told how hard it had been when she was first divorcved, living alone with the children and needing a baby sitter every time she wanted to go out and meet women.

Brenda was almost unbearably moved by the stories. The woman who took thirteen years to come out made her feel less guilty about her own slow process. Envy of the lovers made her want to cry.

There is one story they are not telling, she thought. They are telling about the oppression of silence that isolates us and makes us believe that we are the only lesbians in the world. They are telling about the daily oppression, of not being able to tell neighbors and co-workers about your lover, hiding the most important part of your life. They are not telling about the more direct oppression that physically tears women apart. Perhaps no one else in this room has experienced it.

But they might someday.

I have to tell. I know something and I have to testify. They won't believe me. I can't stand it if they don't believe.

The forum was open now. A woman of about sixty was telling of her discovery that her daughter was a lesbian and of her own desire to support that choice. Several women thanked her and said they wished their mothers had done the same.

I have to testify.

Brenda raised her hand and was called on.

Her voice shook and broke often. "There are other things that happen to lesbians that nobody has talked about. There are many ways that they try to keep us from being free to be lesbians. Sometimes the brainwashing is very literal. Some lesbians are put in mental hospitals. Some are given electric shocks. They gave my lover electric shocks. Every time she thought about loving women she felt a physical pain. She tried going to another therapist to undo what had been done to her, but it was too hard. She couldn't do it. None of us are free if they can do that to us. We have to resist them and help each other. I hope nothing like this happens to any of the rest of you, but it could."

Brenda stopped, overwhelmed by having said this in a public forum.

The room was full of silence. She was sure that none of them—or very few—believed her. They thought she was crazy.

"Are you all right?" one woman asked.

"Yes, I'm all right. I have friends. I'm dealing with it. I just wanted to tell."

All were silent again.

Then another woman raised her hand and told about her problems with her parents.

Whenever any of these women—a significant percentage of the lesbians in this town—sees me again, perhaps she will think I am crazy and avoid me. Or she will think I am in so much pain that she will avoid me anyway.

Lesbians are in mortal danger. They must resist. They don't want to hear that.

The stigma has passed from you to me, Andy. Let all those who would doubt you, doubt me. I don't want any woman who would reject you. I don't want anybody who wouldn't believe what happened.

Let them know me by the shocks. If you are not Andy, then I am.

I shall never stop testifying.

One day in mid-April a letter arrived. It was written in the same new handwriting as the last letter. Bad already called it "religious fanatic handwriting."

Dear Bad,

I am fine and well now. Don't worry about my health.

I am so happy. Jesus has made me so happy. You don't understand how happy. I am happy to be with a group of real Christians.

God plans all things. I know that the doctor who used the shocks was not a good man, but I'm glad that happened to me because it brought me to Jesus. Jesus used the shocks as a warning about my life. Now I have greater peace than I have ever known. I was miserable before because I was sinning, separating myself from Jesus, Christians, and most of the rest of the world.

I have decided not to testify at the trial. My testimony would only hurt innocent people like my family.

I am giving up all associations with that life. I am going to close out the post office box at the end of the month, so don't write there. I am canceling my subscriptions to gay and women's publications. I am not talking to any of my old friends. I am going to break with you completely.

Jesus is showing me a better life. I am lucky to have his blessing.

Karen

She's so far gone that she blesses the shocks. Saved by the holy shocks of God. Thunderbolts from heaven. When they praise their pain, you know you've lost.

Brenda wrote a final letter:

Dear Karen,

You may not testify (I'm afraid I was wrong to try to stop you), but I will. I shall fight the oppression of lesbians all my life. I'll never bless those damn shocks that hurt my baby.

I would go through the same thing all over again. I do not reject the Andys of this world. I give myself to the Andys of this world forever.

Love,
Bad

Brenda knew she would not fling herself at the Andys of this world, however; the mere thought of women who were insecure about their lesbianism was frightening.

She never heard from Andy again.

For the next few years, she sent cards for Andy's birthday and Christmas. She also allowed herself to send a note card saying "occupant is gone. Mouse and I are happy," when Ted finally was persuaded to move out, a few months after the last trip to Cleveland.

After two years, Brenda decided to stop sending cards. Surely Andy would know that she was not forgotten. Perhaps sending the cards was only another way of demonstrating her superior loyalty.

Brenda did not remain celibate forever, either. In the next two years, she had two brief interludes with women.

So Bad, the one who began as a married woman, became an adamant lesbian, while Andy, who had never slept with a man, went straight.

Perhaps she would not write a Ph.D. thesis after all—this story seemed more important.

She was afraid of exposing herself, particularly her racism. No doubt some women would say that she was a racist if she wrote about a black woman who appeared to be dependent on a white woman. Could she write as if Andy were white, and escape the charges? A white woman, too, could be shocked, and the story might be much the same.

No, that was outrageous cowardice. Andy was Andy and could not be changed one iota. She was black and it was not right to turn her into a white woman.

I have to testify, said Brenda. I want to be Bad, and I cannot be Bad without Andy. The two depend on one another.

Finally, Brenda forced herself to sit down and relive the story while she wrote it.

I am not allowed to go to Cleveland.

Publications of
THE NAIAD PRESS, INC.
P.O. Box 10543 • Tallahassee, FL 32302
Mail orders welcome. Please include 15% postage.

To the Cleveland Station by Carol Anne Douglas. A novel.
192 pp. ISBN 0-930044-27-4 — $6.95

The Nesting Place by Sarah Aldridge. A novel. 224 pp.
ISBN 0-930044-26-6 — $6.95

This Is Not for You by Jane Rule. A novel. 284 pp.
ISBN 0-930044-25-8 — $7.95

Faultline by Sheila Ortiz Taylor. A novel. 140 pp.
ISBN 0-930044-24-X — $6.95

The Lesbian in Literature by Barbara Grier. 3rd ed.
Foreword by Maida Tilchen. A comprehensive bibliog.
240 pp. ISBN 0-930044-23-1 — ind. $7.95 / inst. $10.00

Anna's Country by Elizabeth Lang. A novel. 208 pp.
ISBN 0-930044-19-3 — $6.95

Lesbian Writer: Collected Work of Claudia Scott
edited by Frances Hanckel and Susan Windle. Poetry. 128 pp.
ISBN 0-930044-22-3 — $4.50

Prism by Valerie Taylor. A novel. 158 pp.
ISBN 0-930044-18-5 — $6.95

Black Lesbians: An Annotated Bibliography compiled by
JR Roberts. Foreword by Barbara Smith. 112 pp.
ISBN 0-930044-21-5 — ind. $5.95 / inst. $8.00

The Marquise and the Novice by Victoria Ramstetter.
A novel. 108 pp. ISBN 0-930044-16-9 — $4.95

Labiaflowers by Tee A. Corinne. 40 pp. — $3.95

Outlander by Jane Rule. Short stories, essays.
207 pp. ISBN 0-930044-17-7 — $6.95

Sapphistry: The Book of Lesbian Sexuality by
Pat Califia. 195 pp. ISBN 0-930044-14-2 — $6.95

(continued on next page)

Lesbian-Feminism in Turn-of-the-Century Germany.
An anthology. Translated and edited by Lillian Faderman
and Brigitte Eriksson. 120 pp. ISBN 0-930044-13-4 $5.95

The Black and White of It by Ann Allen Shockley.
Short stories. 112 pp. ISBN 0-930044-15-0 $5.95

At the Sweet Hour of Hand-in-Hand by Renée Vivien.
Translated by Sandia Belgrade. Poetry. xix, 81 pp.
ISBN 0-930044-11-8 $5.50

All True Lovers by Sarah Aldridge. A novel. 292 pp.
ISBN 0-930044-10-X $6.95

A Woman Appeared to Me by Renée Vivien. Translated
by Jeannette H. Foster. A novel. xxxi, 65 pp.
ISBN 0-930044-06-1 $5.00

Lesbiana by Barbara Grier. Book reviews from
The Ladder. iv, 309 pp. ISBN 0-930044-05-3 $5.00

Cytherea's Breath by Sarah Aldridge. A novel. 240 pp.
ISBN 0-930044-02-9 $6.95

Tottie by Sarah Aldridge. A novel. 181 pp.
ISBN 0-930044-01-0 $5.95

The Latecomer by Sarah Aldridge. A novel. 107 pp.
ISBN 0-930044-00-2 $5.00